ADA CARTIANU

THE WORLD HAS LOST ITS MIND

A WAKE-UP CALL

A FRANK EXAMINATION OF THE FRACTURES THAT HAVE APPEARED
IN THE FOUNDATION OF OUR POLITICAL LANDSCAPE

THE WORLD HAS LOST ITS MIND
A WAKE-UP CALL
A FRANK EXAMINATION OF THE FRACTURES THAT HAVE APPEARED IN THE FOUNDATION OF OUR POLITICAL LANDSCAPE

Our book may be purchased in bulk.
Please contact your local book seller, Barnes & Noble,
Amazon, RebELLE P.A or Ada Cartianu Art Gallery at
office@adacartianu.com
www.AdaCartianu.com

TABLE OF CONTENTS

PREFACE

We stand at a precipice. A chasm yawns beneath our feet, threatening to swallow the very ground we've built upon – the foundation of our shared world, once seemingly solid, now fractured and groaning under immense strain. Have you felt it? The unsettling tremor, the creeping uncertainty that whispers, "The world has lost its mind"?

This is not hyperbole. This is a reckoning. The principles we once held as self-evident truths – reason, empathy, cooperation, and the pursuit of collective betterment – are being eroded by a rising tide of fear, division, and shortsighted self-interest. The delicate equilibrium of our political systems, painstakingly constructed over generations, is teetering, threatened by forces that seek to dismantle the very institutions designed to protect our freedoms.

This book is not a lament for a bygone era. It is a wake-up call. It is a frank examination of the fractures that have appeared in the foundation of our political landscape – the deep cracks of inequality, the insidious fissures of misinformation, and the gaping chasms of apathy that have allowed the seeds of populism, nationalism, and authoritarianism to take root and flourish.

We will confront the uncomfortable truths about the rise of these forces, understand the seductive appeal they hold, and trace their devastating impact on societies across the globe. But more than that, we will identify the precise points of vulnerability, the weaknesses in the system that have allowed these dangers to manifest.

This is not an endeavor for the faint of heart. It requires a willingness to question deeply held beliefs, to challenge established norms, and to face the uncomfortable reality that the comfort of the status quo is no longer an option.

However, despair is not the answer. For within this crisis lies an opportunity – a chance to rebuild, to reinforce, to create a more resilient and just world. This book is a call to action, a roadmap for reclaiming our collective sanity. It is a guide to understanding the essential role of democratic institutions, the power of civic engagement, and the urgent need to restore faith in the pursuit of progress.

Let us not stand idly by as the world descends further into chaos. Let us instead arm ourselves with knowledge, courage, and an unwavering commitment to the principles of democracy, justice, and equality. Let us rediscover the power of empathy, cultivate the spirit of collaboration, and build a future where reason prevails, and the world, once lost, finds its mind again. This is not a task for others; it is a task for us, for you, for everyone who believes in the possibility of a better tomorrow. Let the work begin.

INTRODUCTION

Friends, fellow travelers on this spinning blue orb, look around you. Do you feel it? The subtle tremor in the foundations of civilization, the unease whispering through the corridors of power? We stand at a precipice, a point where the very ideals that propelled humanity forward – progress, empathy, connection – threaten to be swallowed by a rising tide of fear, division, and a seductive yearning for the 'good old days' that never truly were.

This is not a time for complacency. This is not a time for silence. This is not a time to believe that someone else will bear the burden of safeguarding our collective future. For too long, we have passively watched as reason has been eroded by rhetoric, nuance smothered by slogans, and the very fabric of our shared humanity frayed by the relentless forces of populism and nationalism – forces that promise security through exclusion, strength through conformity, and a false sense of belonging built on the ashes of understanding.

The world has, in a sense, lost its mind. It has succumbed to the siren song of simplistic solutions to complex problems, traded critical thinking for comforting narratives, and allowed the shadows of authoritarianism to lengthen across the landscape. But hope, like a seed buried deep beneath the winter snow, still flickers within us.

It is a hope rooted in the unwavering belief in the power of democracy, the transformative potential of progress, and the undeniable strength we find in our diversity.

This book, *The World Lost Its Mind,* is not a lament for a bygone era. It is a call to arms. It is an invitation to rediscover our collective sanity, to reclaim the values that bind us together, and to rise up against the forces that seek to divide and conquer. It is a journey into the heart of the challenges we face – the rise of dangerous ideologies, the erosion of human rights, the urgent need to protect our freedoms. But more importantly, it is a roadmap towards a future where inclusion triumphs over exclusion, where empathy overcomes apathy, and where the rights and dignity of every individual are not just promised, but fiercely defended.

Let us not be defined by the darkness that threatens to engulf us. Let us be defined by the courage to speak truth to power, the wisdom to embrace complexity, and the unwavering commitment to building a world where every voice can be heard, every perspective valued, and every individual can thrive. The time for silence is over. The time for action is now. Let us, together, help the world find its mind again.

To the dreamers whose visions paint a brighter tomorrow, the rebels whose spirits refuse to be broken, the outcasts who find strength in their individuality, the unconventional thinkers who challenge the boundaries of possibility, the revolutionary hearts that beat with the rhythm of change—this book is for you.

Your voices, your actions, your unwavering belief in the power of good are the seeds of a better world. Let us rise together, and cultivate a future where democracy flourishes and justice prevails.

THE FRACTURING FOUNDATION

Identifying The Cracks In The System

The political landscape is scarred, a clear image to a global crisis that has been quietly, yet relentlessly, eroding the foundations of democratic norms and institutions. From sprawling metropolises to remote villages, the echoes of this crisis reverberate, manifesting in the alarming ascendance of populism, the resurgence of virulent nationalism, the normalization of extremism, and the consolidation of authoritarian tendencies. More concerningly, this confluence of forces fuels a dangerous erosion of the common good, triggering clashes between fundamental human rights and agendas designed to dismantle the very structures that protect them. Examining the unfolding situation in a nation once considered the bedrock of liberal democracy, the United States under a potential second Trump presidency, provides a stark illustration of these global trends and their devastating consequences. This essay will delve into the multifaceted crisis, exploring the specific cracks that have appeared in the American system, and ultimately, highlighting the fragility of democratic ideals in a world increasingly susceptible to the siren song of authoritarianism.

The first, and perhaps most glaring, crack in the American foundation is the deeply entrenched polarization that has metastasized into outright animosity. Driven by partisan media, echo chambers online, and the deliberate cultivation of division by political actors, Americans are increasingly separated not just by differing opinions on policy, but by fundamentally different realities. Shared facts and a common understanding of national identity have become casualties of this ideological warfare. Under the Trump presidency, this polarization would likely intensify. His rhetoric, often designed to provoke and enflame, thrives on division. We could expect a relentless barrage of accusations against his perceived enemies – the "fake news" media, the "radical left," and any institution deemed insufficiently loyal – further widening the chasm between his supporters and detractors. This climate of constant conflict would paralyze legislative efforts, erode trust in government, and potentially lead to increased social unrest and even violence.

Closely linked to polarization is the erosion of trust in key democratic institutions. The media, the justice system, and even scientific consensus have been systematically undermined by targeted disinformation campaigns and the spread of conspiracy theories. This erosion is particularly potent among certain segments of the population, who feel disenfranchised and ignored by the established elites. A second Trump term would likely weaponize this distrust. We could anticipate relentless attacks on the credibility of the courts, particularly if they rule against him or his allies. The independence of the Justice Department would be further threatened, with investigations potentially used as instruments of political retribution. Public confidence in elections, already shaky after 2020, could be further undermined through baseless claims of fraud and renewed efforts to restrict voting rights. The fabric of American democracy relies on the faith of its citizens in these institutions; their continued degradation would represent a significant threat to its survival.

Another critical crack lies in the escalating assault on truth and reason. The proliferation of misinformation and disinformation, fueled by social media algorithms and foreign interference, has created an environment where facts are fungible and conspiracy theories thrive. This "post-truth" era, fueled by appeals to emotion and intuition rather than evidence and logic, makes it increasingly difficult to engage in rational discourse and find common ground. Under a Trump administration, this assault on truth would likely be amplified. We could anticipate the continued dissemination of unsubstantiated claims, the promotion of alternative "facts," and the suppression of dissenting voices within government agencies. The administration's communication strategy would likely focus on manipulating public perception rather than providing accurate information, further blurring the lines between reality and propaganda. This environment of manufactured uncertainty would make it increasingly difficult for citizens to make informed decisions and hold their leaders accountable.

The weakening of democratic norms and traditions represents a significant vulnerability. Unwritten rules of political behavior, such as respect for the separation of powers, the peaceful transfer of power, and the importance of compromise, are increasingly being disregarded in favor of short-term political expediency. This disregard for established norms creates opportunities for abuse of power and undermines the integrity of the democratic process. A second Trump term would likely see a further erosion of these norms. We could anticipate increased executive overreach, attempts to circumvent legal constraints, and a disregard for the independence of Congress. The administration would likely prioritize loyalty over competence in appointments, potentially leading to the politicization of key government positions. This erosion of norms would not only weaken the system of checks and balances but also set a dangerous precedent for future administrations.

The rise of illiberal attitudes within the population poses a subtle yet profound threat. Increasingly, there is a willingness to sacrifice individual liberties and minority rights in the name of security, national unity, or perceived social order. This trend manifests in the growing acceptance of discriminatory policies, the suppression of dissent, and the erosion of freedom of expression. A second Trump presidency would likely exacerbate these illiberal tendencies. We could anticipate renewed efforts to restrict immigration, limit the rights of marginalized groups, and suppress political opposition. The administration's rhetoric would likely appeal to nationalist sentiments and tap into underlying anxieties about cultural change, creating a climate of intolerance and division. This erosion of liberal values would not only undermine the principles of equality and justice but also erode the very foundation of a free and open society.

The United States particularly stands at a critical juncture. The cracks in the foundation of its democratic system, driven by polarization, distrust, the assault on truth, the erosion of norms, and the rise of illiberal attitudes, are widening at an alarming rate. These fissures are not merely theoretical concerns; they represent a tangible threat to the future of American democracy and its ability to serve as a beacon of freedom and justice in an increasingly turbulent world. Addressing these challenges requires a concerted effort to rebuild trust in institutions, promote civil discourse, combat misinformation, uphold democratic norms, and reaffirm the fundamental principles of liberty and equality for all. Failure to do so will inevitably lead to a further fracturing of the system and potentially irreversible damage to the American experiment. The future of democracy, not just in the United States but globally, may well depend on the choices made in the coming years.

The future of democracy appears shrouded in uncertainty, not painted with the bright hues of progress and enlightenment we might have hoped for. Instead, we are witnessing a multifaceted crisis, a slow yet relentless erosion of the democratic norms and institutions that have, for decades, formed the bedrock of stable societies. This crisis is not a singular event but a convergence of interconnected challenges, each amplifying the others to create a potent threat to the principles of self-governance, the rule of law, and the protection of fundamental human rights. At its heart, this erosion stems from the rise of populism, nationalism, extremism, and authoritarianism, all of which are actively chipping away at the foundations of liberal democracy and contributing to a growing tension between individual rights and agendas that seek to dismantle the common good. Understanding the nature of these cracks in the system is crucial to developing effective strategies for defending and revitalizing democratic ideals.

One of the most prominent fissures in this fracturing foundation is the rise of populism. Populist movements, often fueled by economic anxieties, social discontent, and a perceived disconnect between elites and ordinary citizens, capitalize on a sense of grievance and resentment. They typically present a simplified narrative of "us" versus "them," casting themselves as the champions of the "real people" against a corrupt establishment that has betrayed their interests. While populism can, at times, offer a legitimate critique of existing power structures and highlight genuine injustices, its tendency towards demagoguery, the suppression of dissenting voices, and the dismantling of institutional checks and balances poses a significant threat to democratic processes. The allure of a strong leader promising quick fixes and decisive action can be particularly appealing in times of uncertainty, but it often comes at the cost of nuanced debate, compromise, and the protection of minority rights – all essential components of a thriving democracy.

Closely intertwined with populism is the resurgence of nationalism. While a healthy sense of national identity and pride can be a positive force, the exclusionary and often xenophobic forms of nationalism that are gaining traction globally represent a dangerous trend. This brand of nationalism promotes the idea of national superiority, fostering a sense of distrust and hostility towards foreigners, immigrants, and minority groups. It often seeks to rewrite history, glorify the past, and demonize those perceived as threats to national identity. This narrow, inward-looking perspective hinders international cooperation, undermines global institutions, and fuels discriminatory policies that violate fundamental human rights. The rise of nationalist sentiment also provides fertile ground for authoritarian tendencies, as leaders exploit feelings of national vulnerability to justify curtailing civil liberties and consolidating power.

Furthermore, the spread of extremism, both online and offline, further destabilizes the democratic landscape. Extremist ideologies, ranging from far-right white supremacist movements to religiously motivated terrorist groups, thrive in environments of polarization and social fragmentation. They often exploit online platforms to spread propaganda, recruit new members, and incite violence against targeted groups. The anonymity and echo chambers of the internet allow extremist views to proliferate unchecked, radicalizing individuals and normalizing hate speech. This not only poses a direct threat to public safety but also erodes the sense of shared values and mutual respect that is essential for a functioning democracy. The challenge lies in finding effective ways to combat extremism without infringing upon freedom of speech and expression, a delicate balancing act that requires careful consideration and nuanced strategies.

Finally, the most alarming crack in the democratic foundation is the creeping authoritarianism being witnessed in various corners of the globe. This manifests in different forms, from outright dictatorships to "illiberal democracies" where elections are held but civil liberties are restricted, the media is controlled, and the judiciary is compromised. Authoritarian regimes often employ tactics such as disinformation campaigns, gerrymandering, and voter suppression to maintain power and silence dissent. They often target civil society organizations, independent journalists, and human rights defenders, effectively stifling any opposition to their rule. The rise of authoritarianism is not only a tragedy for the citizens living under such regimes but also poses a threat to global stability and security, as authoritarian leaders are often more likely to engage in aggressive foreign policy and undermine international norms.

The convergence of these forces — populism, nationalism, extremism, and authoritarianism — creates a perfect storm that threatens to dismantle the common good, replacing it with a fragmented and unequal society. The core principles of human rights, including freedom of expression, freedom of assembly, and equality before the law, are increasingly challenged by agendas that prioritize national interests, cultural homogeneity, and the suppression of dissent. This clash between universal human rights and particularistic agendas represents a fundamental challenge to the international order and requires a concerted effort to reaffirm the importance of human dignity and the rule of law.

In the sections that follow, we will explore deeper into the specific challenges posed by these trends, examine the mechanisms through which they are undermining democratic norms and institutions, and explore potential strategies for defending and revitalizing democracy in the face of these formidable threats. The future of democracy in 2025 depends on our ability to understand the cracks in the system and to develop effective strategies for repairing the fracturing foundation.

THE BOILING FROG
How We Got Here

Let's explore the slow, creeping erosion of trust in institutions, fueled by economic inequality, globalization, and the rise of social media.

The fable of the boiling frog illustrates a critical danger: the inability to perceive a threat that develops gradually. A frog placed in boiling water will immediately jump out, but one placed in cool water that is slowly heated will remain, oblivious to the mounting peril, until it is too late. This unsettling metaphor resonates powerfully with the current state of society, particularly in understanding the slow, creeping erosion of trust in institutions that once formed the bedrock of our collective identity and stability. This erosion isn't the result of a sudden shock, but rather a gradual warming of the societal pot, fueled by a confluence of factors including burgeoning economic inequality, the disruptive forces of globalization, and the pervasive influence of social media.

One of the most significant contributors to this gradual loss of faith is the widening chasm of economic inequality. For decades, the promise of upward mobility, the cornerstone of the "American Dream" and similar ideals around the world, has been steadily eroding. While productivity has increased, wages for the vast majority have stagnated, and the benefits of economic growth have been disproportionately concentrated at the very top. This disparity breeds resentment and a sense of unfairness, leading individuals to question the legitimacy of systems that seem rigged in favor of the wealthy and powerful. The perception that hard work no longer guarantees a decent life, coupled with the visible extravagance of the elite, fosters a deep distrust in institutions like government, corporations, and even the financial system, all perceived as complicit in perpetuating this inequality. The bailouts of financial institutions during the 2008 crisis, while perhaps necessary to prevent a complete economic collapse, further solidified this perception, as ordinary citizens saw those responsible for the crisis seemingly shielded from its consequences while they themselves faced foreclosure and job losses. This fostered a narrative of "us versus them," undermining the sense of shared purpose and collective well-being necessary for a thriving society.

Globalization, while offering undeniable benefits like increased trade and cultural exchange, has also contributed to this erosion of trust. The outsourcing of jobs to countries with cheaper labor has led to job losses and economic insecurity in developed nations, fueling anxieties about national identity and the future of work. The rise of multinational corporations, often perceived as operating beyond the reach of national laws and regulations, has further exacerbated this sense of powerlessness. Concerns about the exploitation of workers in developing countries, the environmental impact of global supply chains, and the erosion of national sovereignty have all contributed to a growing skepticism towards global institutions and agreements. The complexities of international trade deals, often negotiated behind closed doors, breed suspicion and the feeling that ordinary citizens have little say in decisions that profoundly impact their lives. This perceived lack of control over one's economic destiny fuels a desire for protectionism and a rejection of global cooperation, further undermining trust in established institutions that champion these ideals.

The rise of social media has acted as both a symptom and a catalyst in this process. While offering unparalleled opportunities for connection and information sharing, social media has also become a breeding ground for misinformation, polarization, and echo chambers. The algorithmic amplification of extreme views and conspiracy theories erodes trust in traditional sources of information, like mainstream media and scientific institutions. The anonymity afforded by the internet emboldens individuals to spread hateful rhetoric and engage in online harassment, creating a climate of fear and distrust. The constant bombardment of information, often presented without context or verification, makes it increasingly difficult to discern truth from falsehood, leading to a widespread skepticism towards all forms of authority. Moreover, the performative nature of social media encourages individuals to present curated versions of themselves, further blurring the lines between authenticity and artificiality, and contributing to a general sense of distrust in the motives of others. The constant comparison to others online can also fuel feelings of inadequacy and resentment, exacerbating the sense of economic and social inequality.

The result of these interconnected forces – economic inequality, globalization, and social media – is a society increasingly fragmented and distrustful. Institutions, once seen as pillars of stability and progress, are now viewed with suspicion and cynicism. This erosion of trust has far-reaching consequences, impacting everything from political participation to public health. Citizens who distrust their government are less likely to vote, pay taxes, or comply with regulations. A society riddled with distrust is less resilient in the face of crises, less capable of solving complex problems, and more vulnerable to manipulation and division.

Reversing this trend requires a multifaceted approach. Addressing economic inequality through policies that promote fair wages, affordable healthcare, and access to education is crucial. Fostering greater transparency and accountability in government and corporations can help rebuild trust in institutions. Promoting media literacy and critical thinking skills can empower citizens to navigate the complex information landscape of the digital age. Ultimately, rebuilding trust requires a renewed commitment to civic engagement, empathy, and a shared sense of responsibility for the common good. If we fail to recognize the gradual warming of the societal pot, and fail to act decisively to cool things down, we risk succumbing to the fate of the oblivious frog, boiled alive by our own inaction. Only by acknowledging the complex interplay of these factors and working together to address them can we hope to restore faith in our institutions and build a more just and sustainable future.

THE WHISPERS OF HISTORY
Democratic Decline and the Perils of Complacency

Historical precedents for democratic decline and the dangers of complacency.

Democracy, often hailed as the most just and equitable form of governance, is not an immutable force etched in stone. Its survival is contingent upon constant vigilance, active participation, and a profound understanding of the historical currents that have eroded democratic institutions in the past. To believe that democracy is inherently resistant to decline is to succumb to a dangerous complacency, a complacency that history repeatedly warns against. By examining historical precedents for democratic decay, we can better understand the vulnerabilities inherent in even the most established democratic systems and appreciate the critical importance of safeguarding the principles upon which they are built.

One of the most potent historical illustrations of democratic decline can be found in the twilight years of the Roman Republic. Initially governed by a system of elected officials and representative bodies, the Republic gradually succumbed to internal strife, fueled by widening economic inequality, political polarization, and the ambition of powerful individuals. The Gracchi brothers, reformers who sought to address land distribution inequalities, were assassinated, setting a precedent for political violence. The rise of figures like Marius and Sulla, who commanded the loyalty of their legions and used them to seize power, further destabilized the Republic. The concentration of power in the hands of Julius Caesar, culminating in his dictatorship, marked a decisive turning point. While the forms of republican government persisted for a time, the spirit of civic participation and the balance of power had been irrevocably compromised, paving the way for the autocratic rule of the Roman Empire. The Roman example highlights how unchecked ambition, economic disparities, and the erosion of civic norms can weaken the foundations of a republic, even one as seemingly robust as Rome's.

The Weimar Republic in interwar Germany offers another stark lesson. Established after the First World War, the Weimar Republic was burdened by economic hardship, social unrest, and deep political divisions. The Treaty of Versailles, imposed upon Germany after its defeat, fueled resentment and contributed to a sense of national humiliation. Hyperinflation devastated the German economy, eroding public trust in the government. Extremist political parties, both on the left and the right, gained traction by exploiting popular discontent. The

Nazi Party, led by Adolf Hitler, skillfully manipulated anxieties and promised a return to national greatness. The Weimar constitution, while ostensibly democratic, contained provisions that allowed for the suspension of civil liberties and the consolidation of power in the hands of the president. This loophole was ultimately exploited by Hitler, who, through a combination of electoral success and political maneuvering, dismantled the democratic institutions of the Weimar Republic and established a totalitarian regime. The Weimar Republic serves as a cautionary tale about the fragility of democracy in the face of economic crisis, political polarization, and the rise of demagogic leaders who capitalize on popular grievances.

Beyond these prominent examples, history is replete with instances of democratic backsliding. The decline of democracy in Argentina during the 20th century, the erosion of democratic norms in contemporary Hungary and Poland, and the rise of authoritarian populism in various parts of the world all underscore the persistent threat to democratic institutions. These contemporary examples often involve subtle but significant shifts, such as the manipulation of electoral laws, the suppression of dissent, the weakening of independent judiciaries, and the control of media outlets. These actions, often justified in the name of national security or economic stability, chip away at the foundations of democracy and create an environment in which authoritarianism can flourish.

The danger of complacency lies in the failure to recognize these warning signs and to actively defend democratic principles. Complacency can manifest in several ways: a lack of civic engagement, a decline in voter turnout, a tolerance of political corruption, a failure to hold elected officials accountable, and a general apathy towards the erosion of civil liberties. When citizens become disengaged and disillusioned, they create a vacuum that can be filled by those who seek to undermine democracy.

Furthermore, complacency can lead to the normalization of behaviors and policies that would have previously been considered unacceptable. When the boundaries of acceptable political discourse shift, and when extremist views become increasingly mainstream, the Overton window moves, making it easier for authoritarian ideas to gain traction. The spread of misinformation and disinformation, often amplified by social media, further complicates the situation, making it difficult for citizens to discern truth from falsehood and to make informed decisions.

The history of democratic decline is a powerful reminder that democracy is not a self-sustaining system. It requires constant vigilance, active participation, and a commitment to the principles of freedom, equality, and the rule of law. Complacency is a dangerous enemy of democracy, as it allows the forces of authoritarianism to gain ground and erode the institutions that protect our freedoms. By learning from the mistakes of the past and by actively defending democratic values in the present, we can safeguard the future of democracy and ensure that the whispers of history serve as a warning, not a prophecy. We must remain ever vigilant, for the price of liberty is, indeed, eternal vigilance.

Populism, Nationalism, Extremism, Authoritarianism, Illiberal Democracy

In contemporary political discourse, terms like populism, nationalism, extremism, authoritarianism, and illiberal democracy are frequently invoked to describe and analyze a range of political phenomena. While often used interchangeably, these concepts represent distinct, though sometimes overlapping, ideologies and modes of governance. Understanding their nuances and interrelationships is crucial for navigating the complex political landscape of the 21st century.

Populism, at its core, is a political logic that divides society into two antagonistic groups: "the pure people" and "the corrupt elite." As Cas Mudde argues, populism is an ideology that considers society to be ultimately separated into these two homogeneous and antagonistic groups.. Populist leaders often claim to represent the will of the "common person" and mobilize support by appealing to popular grievances and sentiments. However, populism is not inherently tied to any particular ideology; it can manifest on the left or the right of the political spectrum. For instance, [Insert Example of Left-leaning Populist Leader/Movement] exemplifies left-wing populism by [Explain their key policies and rhetoric], while [Insert Example of Right-leaning Populist Leader/Movement] demonstrates right-wing populism through [Explain their key policies and rhetoric]. Critics argue that populism can be a threat to democratic institutions, as it often simplifies complex issues, disregards minority rights, and undermines the rule of law, while proponents contend that it can be a necessary corrective to unresponsive or elitist political systems.

Nationalism, another potent force in global politics, is an ideology that emphasizes the importance of national identity and loyalty. It posits that the nation should be the primary focus of political allegiance and that national interests should be prioritized above all else. Nationalism takes diverse shapes, ranging from civic nationalism, based on shared values and citizenship, to ethnic nationalism, based on shared ancestry and culture. The French Revolution, with its emphasis on *liberté, égalité, fraternité*, can be seen as an early example of civic nationalism, fostering a sense of collective identity based on shared political ideals. In contrast, 19th and 20th Century German nationalism, with its focus on *Volk* and racial purity, represents a more exclusionary form of ethnic nationalism. While nationalism can foster social cohesion and national pride, it also carries the risk of xenophobia, discrimination, and conflict, particularly when it morphs into more aggressive forms.

Extremism goes beyond simply holding strong opinions; it involves the endorsement of ideas and actions that are far outside the accepted norms of a given society and that often advocate for violence or other illegal means to achieve political goals. Extremist ideologies can be rooted in various sources, including religious fundamentalism, political radicalism, and racial supremacy. For example, [Insert Example of Religious Extremist Group] promotes [Explain their beliefs and actions], while [Insert Example of Political Extremist Group] advocates for [Explain their beliefs and actions]. What is considered "extreme" is often relative and depends on the specific context and prevailing social values. However, extremism generally poses a threat to democratic societies by undermining tolerance, promoting violence, and challenging the legitimacy of established institutions. Furthermore, the line between extremism and legitimate political dissent can be blurry and subject to manipulation.

Authoritarianism is a form of government characterized by strong central power and limited political freedoms. Authoritarian regimes typically suppress dissent, restrict civil liberties, and control the flow of information. Unlike totalitarian regimes, which seek to control every aspect of citizens' lives, authoritarian regimes primarily focus on maintaining political power. Examples of authoritarian states include [Insert Example of Authoritarian Regime] where [Explain its key features and methods of control], and [Insert Another Example of Authoritarian Regime] which demonstrates [Explain how it differs from the first example]. Authoritarianism can arise from various sources, including military coups, popular uprisings, and the erosion of democratic institutions. While some argue that authoritarianism can provide stability and economic development, it often comes at the cost of human rights and political participation.

Illiberal Democracy, a term popularized by Fareed Zakaria, describes regimes that hold elections but fail to uphold key liberal principles such as the rule of law, protection of minority rights, and freedom of speech and assembly. In an illiberal democracy, the government may be elected, but it often uses its power to suppress dissent, manipulate the media, and undermine the independence of the judiciary. [Insert Example of Illiberal Democracy] demonstrates this by [Explain how it restricts civil liberties and undermines democratic norms]. Illiberal democracies pose a challenge to traditional understandings of democracy, as they highlight the importance of not only electoral legitimacy but also the protection of fundamental rights and freedoms. The rise of illiberal democracies raises concerns about the erosion of democratic values and the potential for democratic backsliding.

These five concepts – populism, nationalism, extremism, authoritarianism, and illiberal democracy – are not mutually exclusive; they can interact and reinforce one another in complex ways. For example, a populist leader might exploit nationalist sentiments to gain support for authoritarian policies, while extremist groups might use social media to spread their ideologies and recruit new members. Understanding these interconnections is essential for analyzing the challenges facing democracies around the world and for developing effective strategies to promote democratic values and institutions. [**Insert Thesis Statement Here that connects all these concepts to the main argument you are trying to make in the essay.**]

THE RISE OF REACTION
Populism as a Symptom of Democratic Deficiencies and a Threat to Liberal Values

The surge of populism across the globe is not a spontaneous eruption but a feverish symptom of deeper systemic failures within liberal democracies. While often presented as a revolutionary force offering immediate solutions, populism is more accurately understood as a reactive movement, thriving in the cracks left by unchecked economic inequality, pervasive social alienation, and the perceived failures of established political elites. Its seductive simplicity and promise of direct representation mask a darker side, one that often undermines the very foundations of liberal democracy it claims to be revitalizing.

At its core, populism is a political strategy that pits "the people," a homogenous and often idealized group, against a perceived elite that is accused of being corrupt, self-serving, and out of touch with the concerns of ordinary citizens. This Manichean worldview simplifies complex issues, reduces political discourse to a battle between good and evil, and cultivates resentment towards those deemed to be part of the "establishment." The appeal of this narrative is undeniable, particularly in contexts where economic disparities have widened, and traditional institutions have lost credibility.

The rise of economic inequality is arguably the most significant breeding ground for populism. Decades of neoliberal policies, characterized by deregulation, privatization, and globalization, have concentrated wealth in the hands of a few, leaving many feeling economically insecure and marginalized. The decline of manufacturing industries and the rise of precarious gig work have eroded traditional social safety nets, leaving working-class communities vulnerable and resentful. Populist leaders exploit this economic anxiety by promising to redistribute wealth, protect domestic industries, and "take back" control from global forces that are perceived to be responsible for economic hardship. This economic populism, however, often relies on simplistic solutions like protectionism or unsustainable welfare programs, masking the need for more nuanced and comprehensive reforms to address the root causes of inequality.

Beyond economic grievances, populism thrives on social alienation and a sense of cultural displacement. Rapid social and cultural changes, such as increasing immigration, multiculturalism, and the decline of traditional values, can create anxieties and fears among those who feel their identities and traditions are under threat. Populist leaders tap into these anxieties by promoting a nostalgic vision of the past, emphasizing national identity, and scapegoating minority groups for societal problems. This cultural populism can fuel xenophobia, racism, and other forms of discrimination, further dividing society and undermining social cohesion. For example, the rhetoric surrounding immigration often paints immigrants as a drain on resources and a threat to national security, ignoring the complex realities of migration and the contributions immigrants make to society.

The perceived failures of established political elites to address these underlying issues contribute significantly to the rise of populism. The erosion of trust in institutions such as political parties, mainstream media, and expert opinions creates a vacuum that populists readily fill. Populist leaders often present themselves as outsiders, untainted by the corrupting influence of the establishment, and claim to speak directly for "the people." This anti-establishment rhetoric resonates with those who feel ignored or betrayed by traditional political actors. The ease with which misinformation and conspiracy theories spread online further erodes trust in established institutions and creates an environment where populist narratives can flourish.

However, the seductive appeal of populism masks a darker side that poses a significant threat to liberal democracy. One of the most concerning aspects of populism is its tendency towards authoritarianism and its disregard for democratic norms and institutions. Populist leaders often demonize political opponents, suppress dissent, and undermine the independence of the judiciary and the media. They may also attempt to manipulate electoral processes to consolidate their power and silence dissenting voices. This erosion of democratic checks and balances can lead to a gradual slide towards authoritarianism, undermining the very principles of freedom, equality, and the rule of law.

Another danger of populism is its tendency to scapegoat minority groups and incite social division. By demonizing immigrants, refugees, or other marginalized communities, populist leaders can divert attention from their own failings and consolidate their support among a specific segment of the population. This divisive rhetoric can fuel hate crimes, discrimination, and even violence, undermining social cohesion and creating a climate of fear and intolerance. The rise of anti-immigrant sentiment in many European countries, for example, has been accompanied by an increase in hate speech and attacks against immigrants and asylum seekers.

Moreover, populism often relies on simplistic solutions to complex problems, neglecting the need for evidence-based policymaking and critical thinking. Populist leaders may promise to quickly "fix" problems by implementing radical policies without considering the potential consequences. This disregard for expertise and evidence can lead to ineffective policies that exacerbate existing problems or create new ones. The Brexit referendum, for example, was fueled by populist slogans and promises that failed to materialize, resulting in significant economic and political challenges for the United Kingdom.

The rise of populism is a complex phenomenon that reflects deeper failures in liberal democracies to address economic inequality, social alienation, and a crisis of trust in established institutions. While populism may offer a temporary sense of empowerment to those who feel marginalized and disenfranchised, its divisive rhetoric, authoritarian tendencies, and simplistic solutions pose a significant threat to the long-term health of liberal democracy. Addressing the root causes of populism requires a comprehensive approach that includes tackling economic inequality, promoting social inclusion, restoring trust in institutions, and fostering a more informed and engaged citizenry. Only by addressing these underlying issues can we hope to build a more just and equitable society that is resistant to the seductive allure of populism and capable of upholding the values of freedom, equality, and the rule of law. Ignoring the complex challenges that feed populism risks allowing its dark side to further erode the foundations of democratic societies.

THE DOUBLE-EDGED SWORD
Nationalism, Social Cohesion, and the Seeds of Conflict

Nationalism, a potent ideology and political force, is a complex phenomenon capable of simultaneously fostering profound social cohesion and sowing the seeds of exclusionary practices and international conflict. While its proponents often champion it as a unifying force, essential for national identity and progress, a deeper examination reveals its inherent tensions and potential for regression into dangerous forms of populism. To truly understand nationalism, we must dissect its philosophical underpinnings, analyze its diverse political manifestations, and acknowledge the inherent risk of its descent into a darker, more exclusionary realm.

At its heart, nationalism is a belief in the inherent value and importance of the nation. This belief is typically accompanied by a sense of collective identity, shared history, culture, and often, language. Philosopher Ernest Gellner argued that nationalism is essentially a modern phenomenon, linked to industrialization and the need for standardized communication and education. In this view, the nation is not a primordial entity but a constructed community, forged from shared experiences and a deliberate cultivation of common identity. This construction is often deployed to legitimate political authority and mobilize populations towards shared goals.

From a political perspective, nationalism can manifest in diverse and often contradictory forms. Liberal nationalism, for instance, emphasizes civic participation, individual rights, and the rule of law within a national framework. Idealized by thinkers like John Stuart Mill, it seeks to reconcile national identity with universal values, viewing the nation as a vehicle for promoting progress and international cooperation. This form of nationalism often champions self-determination, allowing nations to govern themselves free from external domination.

However, the allure of national unity can easily morph into a more aggressive and exclusionary form, often termed ethnic or cultural nationalism. This variant prioritizes shared ancestry, cultural heritage, and often, religious affiliation as the defining characteristics of the nation. Membership is often based on immutable characteristics rather than conscious choice, creating a rigid and often discriminatory hierarchy. This form of nationalism can lead to the marginalization and persecution of minorities, the suppression of dissent, and the justification of expansionist policies aimed at uniting "kin" across borders.

The risk of exclusion inherent in nationalism stems from its inherent need to define a boundary, a "we" in contrast to a "them." The very act of defining national identity involves drawing lines, distinguishing between those who belong and those who do not. This distinction can be relatively benign, fostering a sense of shared community and pride. However, it can also be exploited to create fear, resentment, and ultimately, hostility towards those perceived as "outsiders," whether they are immigrants, ethnic minorities, or neighboring nations. This process is often fueled by populist rhetoric that simplifies complex issues, scapegoats vulnerable groups, and appeals to primal emotions of fear and insecurity.

Furthermore, the pursuit of national interests, often framed as the paramount goal of any nation-state, can easily lead to international conflict. The belief that one's nation is superior, coupled with the desire to protect its interests, can justify aggressive actions against other nations, ranging from economic protectionism to military intervention. The history of the 20th century, scarred by two world wars driven in part by virulent forms of nationalism, serves as a stark reminder of the dangers of unchecked national ambition.

The contemporary rise of populism, often intertwined with nationalist sentiments, further exacerbates these risks. Populist leaders often exploit pre-existing anxieties and grievances, promising to restore national greatness and defend national identity against perceived threats. Their rhetoric frequently demonizes immigrants, international institutions, and global elites, reinforcing a sense of victimhood and fueling resentment towards perceived enemies. This combination of nationalism and populism creates a volatile mix, capable of undermining democratic institutions, eroding social cohesion, and escalating international tensions.

The dark side of populism, often fueled by nationalist fervor, lies in its tendency to prioritize the "will of the people," as defined by the populist leader, over established norms of constitutionalism, human rights, and minority protections. This can lead to the erosion of checks and balances, the suppression of dissent, and the persecution of those who challenge the populist leader's authority. The rise of authoritarian regimes throughout history often begins with the mobilization of nationalist sentiments under the banner of populism.

Nationalism is a double-edged sword. It can be a powerful force for social cohesion, national identity, and progress. However, its inherent tendency towards exclusion and its susceptibility to manipulation by populist leaders pose a significant threat to both domestic and international peace and stability. Navigating the complexities of nationalism requires a critical awareness of its potential pitfalls, a commitment to inclusive national identities that embrace diversity, and a firm defense of democratic institutions and the rule of law. Only through such vigilance can we hope to harness the positive aspects of nationalism while mitigating its darker, more destructive tendencies. The challenge for the 21st century is to cultivate a form of nationalism that promotes cooperation and mutual respect, rather than division and conflict. This requires a conscious effort to move beyond the simplistic and often divisive narratives of populism and embrace a more nuanced and inclusive vision of national identity.

THE EROSION OF LIBERTY
Illiberalism, Populism, and the Perils of Democratic Backsliding

The 21st century has witnessed a resurgence of political ideologies that challenge the fundamental tenets of liberal democracy, a system long considered the pinnacle of political evolution. Among these challenges, illiberalism stands out as a particularly insidious threat, offering a seductive yet ultimately corrosive alternative to the established order. Illiberal democracies, while nominally adhering to electoral processes, represent a dangerous step towards authoritarianism by eroding the very institutions that are meant to protect individual rights. They capitalize on popular discontent, often fueled by the dark side of populism, ultimately undermining the foundations of a just and free society.

Illiberalism, at its core, rejects the liberal commitment to individual rights, the rule of law, and the separation of powers. It prioritizes the will of the majority, often interpreted and manipulated by charismatic leaders, above the protection of minority rights and the constraints imposed by constitutional principles. This emphasis on the collective, often framed in terms of national identity and cultural purity, allows illiberal regimes to justify actions that would be unthinkable in a liberal democracy. Freedom of the press, the independence of the judiciary, and the rights of civil society organizations all become targets, seen as obstacles to the fulfillment of the "people's will."

The allure of illiberalism often stems from its promise of decisive action and a return to perceived traditional values. In a world grappling with economic inequality, social fragmentation, and anxieties about globalization, the populist appeal of illiberal leaders can be irresistible. These leaders often portray themselves as outsiders, champions of the common people against a corrupt elite, and offer simplistic solutions to complex problems. They skillfully exploit societal grievances, channeling anger and frustration into a unified, albeit often exclusionary, political force. The promise of a strong leader who can "get things done," unburdened by the constraints of due process and legal procedures, can be particularly appealing to populations disillusioned with the perceived ineffectiveness of traditional political institutions.

However, the "dark side of populism" lies in its inherent susceptibility to manipulation and its tendency to demonize dissenting voices. Illiberal leaders often employ propaganda and disinformation campaigns to cultivate a climate of fear and distrust. They use state-controlled media to propagate their narrative, silencing critics and demonizing opposition as enemies of the state. This systematic suppression of dissent creates a chilling effect, discouraging independent thought and critical analysis. Furthermore, the emphasis on national unity and cultural homogeneity often leads to the persecution of minority groups, who are scapegoated for society's problems and portrayed as threats to the national identity.

One of the most significant threats posed by illiberal democracies is the erosion of the rule of law. Independent judiciaries, the cornerstone of a just and fair society, are often subjected to political pressure and manipulation. Judges are replaced with loyalists, legal precedents are ignored, and the courts become tools for persecuting political opponents. This undermining of the rule of law creates a climate of impunity, where those in power are free to act without fear of accountability. Corruption thrives, and the principles of fairness and equality before the law are abandoned.

The assault on civil society organizations is another key feature of illiberal regimes. NGOs that advocate for human rights, environmental protection, or minority rights are often targeted with restrictive legislation, bureaucratic harassment, and smear campaigns. These organizations are vital for holding governments accountable and promoting democratic values, and their suppression weakens the fabric of civil society and undermines the ability of citizens to participate in public life.

The consequences of illiberalism extend beyond the domestic sphere, impacting international relations and the global order. Illiberal regimes often pursue aggressive foreign policies, challenging international norms and undermining multilateral institutions. They may engage in disinformation campaigns to interfere in the affairs of other countries, support authoritarian regimes, and promote a vision of the world based on national sovereignty and power politics. This erosion of democratic values and the rise of illiberalism pose a significant threat to the stability and prosperity of the international community.

The rise of illiberalism is not inevitable. Countering this trend requires a multifaceted approach that addresses the underlying causes of popular discontent, strengthens democratic institutions, and promotes civic education. Addressing economic inequality, fostering social inclusion, and restoring trust in government are essential for undermining the appeal of populist demagogues. Strengthening the independence of the judiciary, protecting freedom of the press, and supporting civil society organizations are crucial for safeguarding the rule of law and promoting democratic accountability.

Moreover, promoting civic education and critical thinking skills can empower citizens to resist manipulation and propaganda. A well-informed and engaged citizenry is the best defense against the erosion of democratic values. Educating citizens about the importance of individual rights, the rule of law, and the principles of liberal democracy can help to inoculate them against the seductive appeal of illiberalism.

Preserving liberal democracy requires a renewed commitment to its core values, a willingness to defend democratic institutions, and a recognition that the fight for freedom and justice is an ongoing and never-ending struggle. We must remain vigilant against the insidious threat of illiberalism, and work tirelessly to promote a world where individual rights are respected, the rule of law prevails, and democracy flourishes. The future of liberty depends on it.

THE PERILOUS EDGE
A Philosophical and Political Examination of Extremism

Extremism, in its philosophical and political manifestations, extends far beyond simply holding strong or unconventional opinions. While passionate advocacy and fervent belief are hallmarks of a healthy democratic discourse, extremism transcends these boundaries to encompass the endorsement of ideas and actions that fall drastically outside the accepted norms of a given society. Crucially, this often involves the advocacy for, and even the active engagement in, violence, illegal activities, or the systematic suppression of dissenting voices as a means to achieve specific political and ideological goals. Extremist ideologies are rarely organic, spontaneous phenomena; they are cultivated and disseminated, often drawing strength from deep-seated grievances and anxieties within a society. These ideologies can be rooted in diverse and seemingly disparate sources, including religious fundamentalism, political radicalism (both left and right), racial and ethnic supremacy, and even niche interpretations of environmentalism.

To illustrate the multifaceted nature of extremism, consider the example of Al-Qaeda, a religiously motivated extremist group. Al-Qaeda promotes a radical interpretation of Islam that justifies violence against those they deem "infidels" or enemies of their faith. Their actions, which include terrorist attacks targeting civilians and military personnel alike, are predicated on a belief in the necessity of establishing a global Caliphate governed by their strict interpretation of Sharia law. This objective, coupled with their willingness to employ indiscriminate violence, places them firmly within the realm of religious extremism. Conversely, consider the example of Antifa, a loosely affiliated network of anti-fascist activists. While their stated aim is to combat fascism and white supremacy, some factions within Antifa advocate for, and engage in, property damage, physical confrontations, and the disruption of public gatherings deemed to promote hateful ideologies. Their actions, justified by the belief that violence is necessary to prevent the spread of fascism, demonstrate a form of political extremism on the left of the political spectrum. These examples highlight the diversity and complexity of the ideologies that fuel extremism, demonstrating that it is not confined to any single political or religious perspective.

The very definition of "extreme," however, is often relative and contingent upon the specific socio-political context and prevailing social values of a given society. What might be considered radical or fringe in one era or culture could be viewed as mainstream or even progressive in another. For example, the abolitionist movement of the 19th century, advocating for the complete emancipation of slaves, was considered extreme by many at the time, particularly in the Southern United States. Today, however, the movement is widely recognized as morally justified and historically significant in the fight for human rights. This historical perspective highlights the importance of critical analysis and nuanced understanding when labeling an ideology as "extreme." It necessitates a careful examination of the underlying principles, the potential consequences of its implementation, and the specific context in which it operates.

Despite the contextual nature of its definition, extremism generally poses a significant threat to democratic societies. Its inherent intolerance of dissenting viewpoints undermines the very foundation of open and respectful dialogue that is essential for a healthy democracy. By promoting violence and encouraging the demonization of opposing viewpoints, extremism erodes the principles of pluralism and compromise that are crucial for the functioning of democratic institutions. Furthermore, extremist groups often seek to delegitimize established institutions, portraying them as corrupt, ineffective, or even inherently oppressive. This undermines public trust in government, law enforcement, and the judiciary, making it more difficult for these institutions to maintain order and uphold the rule of law. In extreme cases, this erosion of trust can lead to social unrest, political instability, and even the collapse of democratic governance.

Furthermore, the line separating extremism from legitimate political dissent and robust activism can be dangerously blurry and, crucially, subject to manipulation by actors with ulterior motives. Governments, political parties, and even individuals may strategically label opposing viewpoints as "extreme" in an attempt to silence dissent, discredit their opponents, and consolidate their own power. This tactic, often employed during times of political polarization or social unrest, can have a chilling effect on free speech and open debate, effectively stifling the very democratic processes it purports to protect. Similarly, those who genuinely seek positive social change through passionate advocacy may inadvertently cross the line into extremism if their actions involve violence, intimidation, or the suppression of opposing viewpoints. Therefore, vigilance, critical thinking, and a steadfast commitment to the principles of tolerance, due process, and respect for the rule of law are essential in navigating the complex and often treacherous terrain between legitimate political dissent and the perilous edge of extremism. Understanding the nuances of extremism, its diverse manifestations, and its potential consequences is paramount to safeguarding the principles of a free and democratic society.

Authoritarianism is a form of government characterized by strong central power and limited political freedoms. It represents a significant departure from democratic ideals, prioritizing order and control over individual liberties and participatory governance. Authoritarian regimes typically suppress dissent, restrict civil liberties, and control the flow of information, creating an environment where opposition voices are silenced and the ruling power remains unchallenged. Unlike totalitarian regimes, which seek to control every aspect of citizens' lives, from their thoughts and beliefs to their social interactions and economic activities, authoritarian regimes primarily focus on maintaining political power. While the lines can sometimes blur, the key distinction lies in the *scope* of control. Totalitarianism aims for total societal transformation and conformity, while authoritarianism is more concerned with preserving the existing power structure, even if it allows for some degree of social or economic freedom outside the explicitly political realm.

Examples of authoritarian states illustrate the diverse ways in which this form of government can manifest. Consider, for example, the Authoritarian Regime 20th Century Chile under Augusto Pinochet where the military seized power in a coup, violently suppressing leftist movements and political opponents. Its key features included a brutal secret police force (DINA) that engaged in widespread torture, disappearances, and extrajudicial killings. Freedom of speech and assembly were curtailed, the press was heavily censored, and political parties were banned or severely restricted. The regime justified its actions as necessary to combat communism and maintain national security, often employing nationalist rhetoric to garner support, particularly among conservative segments of society and the business elite. Economically, Pinochet's regime implemented neoliberal policies, leading to significant economic growth for some, but also increased inequality and social unrest, which were met with further repression.

The 20th century offers numerous examples of such authoritarian regimes, including Chile under the rule of Augusto Pinochet from 1973 to 1990. Pinochet's rise to power through a violent military coup against the democratically elected government of Salvador Allende exemplifies the ruthless seizure of power often seen in authoritarian contexts. Once in control, Pinochet established a military junta that systematically dismantled democratic institutions. Congress was dissolved, political parties were banned or severely restricted, and freedom of expression was curtailed. A key characteristic of Pinochet's regime, and of many authoritarian states, was the systematic suppression of dissent. This involved widespread surveillance, the use of torture against political opponents, and extrajudicial killings. The Rettig Report, commissioned after the return to democracy, documented thousands of cases of human rights violations, providing stark evidence of the brutality employed to silence opposition. Furthermore, Pinochet's regime exerted strict control over the media, censoring news and information to maintain its grip on power and propagate a narrative favorable to the government. This control extended to education, where curricula were revised to promote a nationalistic and anti-communist ideology. While initially implementing shock-therapy neoliberal economic policies, pushed by the "Chicago Boys", that created great economic imbalances, the regime also took steps to ensure a level of stability, further legitimizing the authoritarian government in the eyes of some. The Chilean example under Pinochet vividly demonstrates the defining features of authoritarianism: concentrated power, suppression of dissent, and control of information, all employed to maintain the regime's iron grip on society.

Alternatively, the Authoritarian Regime of Modern-day Singapore offers a contrasting example. While Singapore boasts a highly developed economy and relatively high standards of living, it also operates under a system of what some scholars call "soft authoritarianism" or "illiberal democracy." The People's Action Party (PAP) has been in power since independence, consistently winning elections that are often criticized for being less than free and fair due to restrictions on media freedom, gerrymandering, and the use of defamation laws to silence critics. Unlike Pinochet's Chile, Singapore's authoritarianism is often portrayed as pragmatic and efficient, focusing on economic development and social order. However, this comes at the cost of genuine political pluralism and robust protection of civil liberties. Dissent is often stifled through subtle means, such as bureaucratic obstacles, financial penalties, and social pressure, rather than overt violence and repression. This demonstrates how authoritarianism can be maintained through a combination of economic success, social control, and legal maneuvering rather than solely through brute force.

While Singapore boasts a highly developed economy and relatively high standards of living, it also operates under a system of what some scholars call "soft authoritarianism" or "illiberal democracy." This model prioritizes economic development and social stability, often at the expense of certain political and civil liberties.

Unlike traditional authoritarian regimes characterized by overt repression and widespread violence, Singapore's government maintains order through a combination of subtle control, strict regulations, and the enforcement of laws that, while not always draconian, create a climate of self-censorship and discourage dissent. For example, the Internal Security Act (ISA) allows for detention without trial in cases deemed a threat to national security, a power that, while rarely invoked in recent times, remains a significant constraint on freedom of expression and assembly. Furthermore, defamation laws are rigorously enforced, often resulting in substantial damages awarded to government officials and members of the ruling People's Action Party (PAP) in libel suits against critics, effectively silencing opposition voices and inhibiting investigative journalism. Public protests and gatherings are heavily regulated and require permits that are often difficult to obtain for those critical of the government.

The PAP (People's Action Party), which has been in power since 1959, maintains a dominant position in the political landscape. While elections are held regularly, the playing field is often perceived as uneven. The Group Representation Constituencies (GRCs), designed to ensure minority representation in Parliament, have also been criticized for potentially diluting the strength of opposition parties. Furthermore, the government's control over the media landscape, including state-owned newspapers and television channels, ensures that the ruling party's narrative is consistently promoted while alternative viewpoints receive limited exposure. This control extends to online spaces, where the government actively monitors and regulates content, particularly that which is deemed to incite social unrest or challenge the established order.

Proponents of Singapore's model argue that its unique approach to governance has been instrumental in its remarkable economic success and social cohesion. They contend that strong leadership and a focus on long-term planning, unencumbered by the gridlock and instability often seen in more democratic systems, have allowed Singapore to overcome its initial disadvantages and become a global economic powerhouse. They also emphasize the importance of maintaining social harmony in a multi-ethnic and multi-religious society, arguing that strict regulations are necessary to prevent the emergence of divisive forces. The emphasis on meritocracy and education is also presented as a key factor in Singapore's success, with the government arguing that a focus on developing human capital is essential for continued prosperity. Furthermore, the government frequently points to the high levels of public trust and satisfaction with government services as evidence of the legitimacy and effectiveness of its approach.

However, critics argue that Singapore's success has come at a considerable cost to individual freedoms and democratic principles. They point to the limitations on freedom of expression, assembly, and association as evidence of a system that stifles dissent and discourages critical thinking. The lack of a robust and independent civil society is also a concern, as it limits the ability of citizens to hold the government accountable. Furthermore, some argue that the emphasis on economic development has overshadowed the importance of social justice and equality, leading to widening income disparities and a growing sense of alienation among certain segments of the population. The long-term sustainability of Singapore's model is also questioned, with concerns raised about its ability to adapt to a rapidly changing global landscape and the increasing demands for greater political participation from a more educated and globally connected citizenry. Ultimately, Singapore presents a complex case study of a nation that has achieved remarkable economic success while navigating the delicate balance between development, stability, and individual liberties. The debate over whether its "soft authoritarian" model is a viable and justifiable path for other developing nations continues to be a subject of ongoing discussion and scrutiny.

Authoritarianism can arise from various sources, including military coups, as seen in the case of Chile; popular uprisings, where revolutionary movements consolidate power and establish authoritarian rule; and the gradual erosion of democratic institutions, where elected leaders exploit loopholes in the system to amass power and undermine checks and balances. Economic crises, political instability, and social divisions can also create fertile ground for authoritarian movements to gain traction, promising stability and strong leadership in times of uncertainty.

While some argue that authoritarianism can provide stability and economic development, particularly in contexts where democratic institutions are weak or ineffective, it often comes at the cost of human rights and political participation. The suppression of dissent and restriction of civil liberties stifle innovation, creativity, and critical thinking, ultimately hindering long-term social and economic progress. Furthermore, the lack of accountability and transparency inherent in authoritarian regimes can lead to corruption, abuse of power, and a decline in the rule of law. The absence of free and fair elections and the suppression of independent media prevent citizens from holding their leaders accountable, creating a system ripe for exploitation and injustice.

Moreover, the long-term stability of authoritarian regimes is often questionable. While they may appear stable on the surface, the underlying tensions and grievances caused by the suppression of dissent can eventually erupt into social unrest and political upheaval. The lack of legitimate channels for expressing discontent can lead to violent protests and revolutions, destabilizing the regime and potentially plunging the country into chaos. Therefore, while authoritarianism may offer short-term stability, it often does so at the expense of long-term peace, prosperity, and justice. The trade-off between order and liberty remains a central dilemma in political philosophy, and the study of authoritarianism highlights the potential dangers of prioritizing the former over the latter. It is a complex phenomenon with varied manifestations and consequences, demanding careful analysis and critical evaluation of its justifications and impacts.

THE ECONOMICS OF DISCONTENT
Fueling the Fire

Let's analyze the impact of neoliberal policies, automation, and globalization on working-class communities.

Neoliberal policies, automation, and globalization have transformed the world's economies and societies in profound ways. While these forces have brought about unprecedented wealth and technological progress, they have also left many working-class communities feeling marginalized, disenfranchised, and discontented. In this essay, we will analyze the impact of these trends on working-class communities and explore the need for a progressive alternative to address the economic and social challenges they face.

Neoliberalism and the Rise of Inequality

Neoliberalism, a philosophy that emphasizes the role of the free market and individual freedom, has been the dominant economic ideology since the 1980s. However, the implementation of neoliberal policies, such as deregulation, privatization, and tax cuts for the wealthy, has led to a significant increase in income and wealth inequality. The rich have gotten richer, while the middle and working classes have seen their wages stagnate and their economic security decline.

The erosion of the social safety net and the decline of labor protections have further exacerbated these trends. In many countries, workers have fewer rights and less bargaining power than they did decades ago, making it difficult for them to secure decent wages and benefits. As a result, many working-class families are struggling to make ends meet, despite being employed in full-time jobs.

Automation and the Threat to Jobs

Alongside neoliberalism, automation and globalization have also played a significant role in reshaping the labor market. Automation, in particular, has led to the loss of millions of jobs, as machines and algorithms replace human workers in many industries. While automation can bring about increased productivity and efficiency, it also poses a significant threat to job security and social stability.

The displacement of workers by automation can have far-reaching consequences, such as increased poverty, social unrest, and political instability. Moreover, the transition to a more automated economy may exacerbate existing inequalities, as the benefits of automation are often not evenly distributed. In many cases, the owners of capital and technology reap the majority of the gains, while workers bear the costs.

Globalization
and the Race to the Bottom

Globalization, the process of increasing economic, political, and cultural integration among countries, has brought about many benefits, such as increased trade, investment, and cross-cultural understanding. However, it has also led to a race to the bottom in terms of labor standards, wages, and social protections.

In many countries, multinational corporations have taken advantage of weak labor laws and lax environmental regulations to produce goods at lower costs. This has resulted in the exploitation of workers, particularly in the Global South, and the degradation of the environment. Moreover, the competition for foreign investment has led many governments to prioritize the interests of multinational corporations over those of their own citizens, further weakening labor protections and social welfare systems.

The Need for a Progressive Alternative

To address the economic and social challenges facing working-class communities, a progressive alternative to neoliberalism is necessary. This alternative should prioritize the well-being of people and the planet over the interests of capital and technology.

Some key principles of a progressive alternative include:

- **Strengthening labor protections** and social welfare systems to ensure that all workers have access to decent wages, benefits, and working conditions.

- **Investing in education**, training, and job creation programs to help workers transition to new industries and occupations.

- **Promoting economic democracy** and worker ownership to give workers a greater say in the decisions that affect their lives and communities.

- **Implementing progressive taxation** and public spending policies to reduce income and wealth inequality.

- **Strengthening international cooperation** and regulation to ensure that globalization benefits all countries and peoples, rather than just a select few.

Neoliberal policies, automation, and globalization have fueled the fire of discontent among working-class communities, exacerbating existing inequalities and undermining social stability. To address these challenges, a progressive alternative that prioritizes the well-being of people and the planet is necessary. By strengthening labor protections, investing in education and job creation, promoting economic democracy, implementing progressive taxation and public spending policies, and strengthening international cooperation, we can build a more equitable and sustainable economy that works for all.

Let's explore the widening gap between the rich and the poor and its connection to political polarization.

The widening chasm between the rich and the poor is more than just a statistic; it is a smoldering ember beneath the surface of modern society, capable of igniting widespread discontent and fueling the flames of political polarization. While economic inequality has always existed in some form, the increasingly disproportionate distribution of wealth in recent decades, coupled with stagnating wages for many, has created a breeding ground for resentment, frustration, and ultimately, a deep distrust of established institutions. This essay will explore the multifaceted ways in which this economic disparity contributes to the rise of divisive politics, eroding social cohesion and threatening the stability of democratic systems.

One of the most significant consequences of economic inequality is the erosion of trust in government and other societal pillars. When individuals perceive that the system is rigged in favor of the wealthy and powerful, they become less likely to believe in the fairness of elections, the integrity of the justice system, or the impartiality of regulatory bodies. This cynicism, fueled by anecdotal evidence of corporate bailouts, lenient treatment of white-collar crime, and the undue influence of money in politics, breeds a sense of powerlessness and resentment. This is particularly potent when coupled with the feeling that hard work no longer guarantees upward mobility, creating a sense of hopelessness that can drive individuals towards radical or extremist ideologies.

Additionally, economic inequality directly impacts people's lived experiences, leading to vastly different realities based on socioeconomic status. The wealthy have access to superior education, healthcare, and opportunities, allowing them to perpetuate their advantages across generations. Conversely, those struggling to make ends meet face a constant barrage of challenges, including inadequate housing, food insecurity, and limited access to quality education and healthcare for themselves and their children. This disparity in lived experiences fosters a lack of empathy and understanding between different socioeconomic groups. It becomes increasingly difficult for those living in affluent bubbles to comprehend the struggles of those mired in poverty, and vice versa. This disconnect contributes to the formation of echo chambers, where individuals are primarily exposed to information and perspectives that reinforce their existing biases, further exacerbating political divisions.

The rise of globalization and technological advancements, while contributing to economic growth overall, have also played a significant role in widening the wealth gap. The automation of many jobs, coupled with the outsourcing of labor to countries with lower wages, has led to job losses and wage stagnation for a significant portion of the population in developed nations. These displaced workers often feel betrayed by the promises of globalization, which were meant to bring prosperity to all. Instead, they perceive it as a force that has enriched the elite while leaving them behind. This sense of economic insecurity makes them vulnerable to populist rhetoric that scapegoats immigrants, minorities, and other "outsiders" for their economic woes, further fueling the flames of political polarization.

Also, economic inequality can be exploited by political actors seeking to gain or maintain power. Populist leaders often capitalize on the grievances of those feeling economically disenfranchised by promising radical solutions and demonizing the "establishment" that they claim is responsible for their struggles. This can lead to the erosion of democratic norms and institutions, as these leaders often prioritize their own power over the rule of law and the protection of minority rights. By stoking resentment and division, they can effectively mobilize a base of support and undermine the ability of opposing viewpoints to gain traction.

The solutions to addressing the economics of discontent are complex and multifaceted, requiring a concerted effort from governments, businesses, and individuals. Policy interventions such as progressive taxation, increased minimum wages, investments in education and job training, and stronger social safety nets are crucial in leveling the playing field and providing opportunities for upward mobility. Furthermore, addressing the underlying causes of economic inequality, such as the decline of unions and the increasing concentration of corporate power, is essential for creating a more equitable and sustainable economic system.

However, policy solutions alone are not enough. Cultivating empathy, fostering dialogue across socioeconomic divides, and promoting media literacy are also crucial in bridging the gap between different groups and reducing political polarization. Education plays a vital role in helping individuals understand the complex interplay of economic, social, and political forces that contribute to inequality. By equipping citizens with the critical thinking skills necessary to evaluate information and identify manipulative rhetoric, we can inoculate them against the divisive tactics employed by populist leaders and promote a more informed and engaged citizenry.

The economics of discontent is a powerful force shaping the political landscape of the 21st century. The widening gap between the rich and the poor is not just an economic issue; it is a social, political, and moral one that threatens the very fabric of democratic societies. By understanding the complex ways in which economic inequality fuels political polarization, we can begin to address the underlying causes of this discontent and work towards creating a more just, equitable, and stable world for all. This requires a commitment to policies that promote economic opportunity and social mobility, as well as a renewed emphasis on fostering empathy, understanding, and critical thinking amongst all members of society. Only by addressing both the economic and social dimensions of this challenge can we effectively douse the flames of discontent and build a more inclusive and resilient future.

Let's discuss the legitimate grievances of forgotten populations exploited by populist narratives.

The rise of populism across the globe is often attributed to xenophobia, cultural anxieties, or the machinations of charismatic demagogues. While these factors undoubtedly play a role, dismissing the phenomenon without acknowledging the deep-seated economic grievances that fuel it is a dangerous oversimplification. At its core, populist sentiment thrives in the fertile ground of economic discontent, nurtured by the legitimate frustrations of forgotten populations who feel left behind by globalization, technological advancements, and increasingly unequal distribution of wealth. These are the communities whose livelihoods have been eroded, whose voices have been ignored, and whose hopes for a brighter future have been systematically diminished. It is from this wellspring of economic despair that populist narratives draw their power and resonance.

For decades, a narrative of progress and prosperity has dominated the political landscape. However, this narrative often fails to reflect the lived realities of a significant segment of the population. Globalization, while beneficial in many ways, has led to the offshoring of manufacturing jobs, decimating industries and leaving entire communities struggling to adapt. The relentless march of automation, while increasing efficiency and productivity, has displaced workers whose skills are no longer in demand. And while the wealthy have reaped the rewards of these changes, the majority have seen their wages stagnate, their job security diminish, and their opportunities for upward mobility dwindle. This widening gap between the haves and have-nots creates a palpable sense of injustice and breeds resentment towards the perceived beneficiaries of the system.

The impact of these economic shifts is particularly acute in regions that were once the engines of industrial prosperity. The decline of manufacturing hubs in the American Rust Belt, for instance, has left behind a legacy of unemployment, poverty, and social decay. Similar patterns can be observed in former mining towns in Europe and other regions that have experienced a significant decline in traditional industries. These communities, often located in rural or isolated areas, feel forgotten and ignored by the political elite, who are perceived as being more concerned with the needs of urban centers and global corporations. The resulting sense of alienation and marginalization makes them particularly susceptible to populist appeals that promise to restore their lost glory and give them a voice in the political process.

Populist narratives skillfully exploit these anxieties by offering simplistic solutions to complex problems. They often identify scapegoats, such as immigrants or foreign countries, as the source of economic woes, diverting attention from the underlying structural issues. They promise to bring back jobs, protect domestic industries, and restore national pride, often through protectionist policies and nationalist rhetoric. While these promises may be unrealistic or even harmful in the long run, they resonate with those who feel that the existing political system has failed them. The allure of a strong leader who claims to understand their struggles and promises to fight for their interests is particularly powerful in times of economic uncertainty.

Furthermore, the erosion of social safety nets has exacerbated the economic vulnerability of these forgotten populations. Cuts to social programs, declining access to affordable healthcare and education, and the weakening of labor unions have left many individuals and families struggling to make ends meet. Without adequate support from the government or other institutions, they are more susceptible to economic shocks, such as job loss or illness, and less able to adapt to changing economic conditions. This sense of insecurity and vulnerability further fuels the anger and resentment that underpins populist sentiment.

The role of technology in exacerbating economic inequality also cannot be overlooked. The rise of the gig economy, characterized by precarious employment and a lack of benefits, has created a new class of workers who are struggling to make a living. The concentration of wealth in the hands of a few tech giants has further widened the gap between the rich and the poor. And the spread of misinformation and conspiracy theories online has made it more difficult to have informed and rational discussions about economic policy.

Addressing the economic grievances that fuel populism requires a multifaceted approach that goes beyond simplistic solutions and empty promises. It requires a commitment to investing in education and training programs that equip workers with the skills they need to succeed in the 21st-century economy. It requires strengthening social safety nets to provide a cushion for those who are struggling to adapt to changing economic conditions. It requires reforming the tax system to ensure that the wealthy pay their fair share. And it requires promoting policies that foster inclusive growth and ensure that the benefits of economic progress are shared more equitably.

Ultimately, combating populism requires a genuine effort to address the legitimate concerns of forgotten populations and to restore their faith in the political system. It requires listening to their voices, understanding their struggles, and working together to create a more just and equitable society. Ignoring the economic roots of discontent will only allow the fire of populism to continue to burn, consuming the foundations of democracy and threatening the stability of societies around the world. It is only by addressing the underlying economic anxieties that we can hope to quell the flames and build a more inclusive and prosperous future for all.

THE ECHO CHAMBER EFFECT
The Rise of Misinformation

Let's explore the role of social media in amplifying extremist voices and spreading misinformation.

In the digital age, information flows at an unprecedented speed, connecting individuals from all corners of the globe. While this interconnectedness holds immense potential for progress and collaboration, it has also fostered an environment ripe for the proliferation of misinformation and the amplification of extremist voices. This phenomenon, often referred to as the "echo chamber effect," describes the situation where individuals are primarily exposed to information and opinions that reinforce their existing beliefs, creating a closed loop that can hinder critical thinking and contribute to societal polarization. Social media, in particular, plays a significant role in amplifying these echo chambers, contributing to the rise and spread of misinformation in ways that demand critical examination.

The architecture of many social media platforms is inherently conducive to the echo chamber effect. Algorithms, designed to enhance user engagement, prioritize content based on past interactions, creating personalized feeds that tend to show users what they already agree with. This "filter bubble," as it is sometimes called, limits exposure to diverse perspectives and reinforces pre-existing biases. Users are more likely to encounter content from like-minded individuals, often sharing similar political views, cultural beliefs, or consumer preferences. This creates a comfortable, yet ultimately limiting, environment where dissenting opinions are often filtered out or actively dismissed.

The anonymity afforded by the internet, coupled with the ease of sharing content, allows misinformation to spread rapidly and widely. Individuals can create and disseminate false or misleading information without fear of immediate repercussions, and this information can quickly gain traction through social media networks. The speed at which misinformation spreads makes it difficult to counter, even with fact-checking initiatives and debunking efforts. Before accurate information can gain traction, the initial false or misleading content may have already reached a vast audience, shaping their perceptions and potentially impacting their behavior.

The amplification of extremist voices is another significant consequence of the echo chamber effect. Social media platforms provide a space for extremist groups and individuals to connect with like-minded individuals, recruit new members, and spread their ideologies. Within these closed online communities, extremist views are normalized and reinforced, often leading to radicalization and even real-world violence. The anonymity of the internet can also embolden extremist individuals, allowing them to express hateful or violent rhetoric without fear of immediate consequences. The algorithms of social media platforms, in their drive to maximize engagement, can inadvertently amplify extremist content, exposing it to a wider audience and further contributing to its spread.

The consequences of the echo chamber effect and the spread of misinformation are far-reaching. They can erode trust in institutions, fuel political polarization, and even incite violence. When individuals are primarily exposed to information that confirms their existing beliefs, they become less likely to engage in critical thinking or to consider alternative perspectives. This can lead to a hardening of opinions and a decreased willingness to compromise or collaborate with those who hold different views. In a democratic society, this can undermine the ability to engage in constructive dialogue and to find common ground on important issues.

Moreover, the spread of misinformation can have serious consequences for public health, safety, and security. During the COVID-19 pandemic, for example, widespread misinformation about the virus and vaccines contributed to vaccine hesitancy and hindered efforts to control the spread of the disease. Similarly, misinformation about political candidates or electoral processes can undermine trust in elections and fuel political instability.

Addressing the echo chamber effect and combating the spread of misinformation requires a multi-faceted approach. Social media platforms have a responsibility to address the algorithmic biases that contribute to the creation of echo chambers. This could involve modifying algorithms to prioritize diverse perspectives and to limit the spread of misinformation. It also requires investing in robust fact-checking initiatives and developing strategies to counter the spread of false or misleading information.

However, social media platforms cannot solve this problem alone. Individuals also have a responsibility to be critical consumers of information and to seek out diverse perspectives. This involves being aware of the echo chamber effect and actively seeking out information from a variety of sources. It also involves being willing to challenge one's own beliefs and to engage in constructive dialogue with those who hold different views.

Education plays a crucial role in equipping individuals with the critical thinking skills necessary to navigate the complex information landscape of the digital age. By teaching students how to evaluate sources, identify biases, and think critically about information, we can empower them to become more discerning consumers of information and to resist the influence of misinformation.

The echo chamber effect represents a significant challenge in the digital age. Social media plays a crucial role in amplifying extremist voices and spreading misinformation, contributing to societal polarization and undermining trust in institutions. Addressing this challenge requires a multi-faceted approach that involves social media platforms, individuals, and educational institutions. By working together, we can create a more informed and engaged citizenry, capable of critical thinking and resistant to the influence of misinformation. Failing to do so risks further fragmentation of society and a deepening of the divisions that threaten the foundations of democracy.

Let's discuss the breakdown of traditional media and the rise of partisan news sources.

In an increasingly interconnected world, the flow of information has become a defining characteristic of modern life. Yet, this abundance of data presents a paradox: while we have access to more information than ever before, the prevalence of misinformation and the reinforcement of pre-existing beliefs, often referred to as the "echo chamber effect," are on the rise. This phenomenon, fueled by algorithms, social media, and the splintering of the media landscape, poses a significant threat to informed public discourse and a shared understanding of reality. A critical factor contributing to the proliferation of echo chambers is the breakdown of traditional media's dominance and the concurrent rise of partisan news sources.

For decades, traditional media outlets, such as established newspapers, broadcast networks, and reputable news magazines, served as gatekeepers of information. These institutions, while not without their biases, generally adhered to journalistic standards of objectivity, fact-checking, and presenting multiple perspectives. They aimed to provide a common ground of factual information upon which public debates could be based. However, several converging factors have eroded the authority and reach of these traditional sources.

One primary driver of this decline is the fragmentation of the media market. The advent of the internet and the proliferation of cable television channels created an unprecedented array of choices for consumers. No longer were individuals limited to a handful of news sources; instead, they could curate their information diet from a vast and diverse pool, ranging from established news organizations to independent blogs and social media feeds. This, in itself, is not inherently negative. However, the sheer volume of information, coupled with the demands of a 24/7 news cycle, has placed immense pressure on traditional media to compete for attention.

The economic pressures facing traditional media have further exacerbated the problem. Declining readership and viewership have led to reduced advertising revenue, forcing news organizations to cut staff, consolidate resources, and, in some cases, prioritize sensationalism over in-depth reporting. This erosion of journalistic capacity has made it more difficult for traditional media to maintain its role as a reliable source of information and to effectively combat the spread of misinformation.

The rise of partisan news sources has fundamentally altered the media landscape. These outlets, often explicitly aligned with a particular political ideology, prioritize advocacy over objectivity. They cater to specific audiences, reinforcing their pre-existing beliefs and often demonizing opposing viewpoints. While partisan media has always existed, the internet has provided these sources with unprecedented reach and influence. Websites, social media accounts, and online video channels dedicated to promoting a particular political agenda have become increasingly popular, drawing viewers away from traditional news organizations.

The algorithms that power social media platforms and search engines play a crucial role in amplifying the echo chamber effect created by partisan news. These algorithms are designed to personalize user experiences, showing individuals content that they are likely to engage with. This often means prioritizing content that confirms their existing beliefs and filtering out information that challenges them. As a result, users are increasingly exposed to a curated stream of information that reinforces their worldview, creating a self-reinforcing cycle of confirmation bias.

The consequences of the echo chamber effect are far-reaching. When individuals are primarily exposed to information that confirms their beliefs, they become less open to considering alternative perspectives and more resistant to evidence that contradicts their views. This can lead to increased polarization, making it more difficult to find common ground and engage in constructive dialogue. In extreme cases, the echo chamber effect can contribute to the spread of conspiracy theories and extremist ideologies, as individuals become increasingly isolated within their own information bubbles.

Moreover, the erosion of trust in traditional media, coupled with the rise of partisan news sources, has created a climate of widespread skepticism and distrust. It becomes increasingly difficult for individuals to discern between credible information and misinformation, leading to a general erosion of faith in institutions and expertise. This, in turn, can undermine democratic processes and make it more difficult to address complex social and political challenges.

Addressing the echo chamber effect and combating the spread of misinformation requires a multi-faceted approach. Media literacy education is crucial, empowering individuals to critically evaluate information sources and identify bias. Algorithms need to be designed in a way that promotes diversity of viewpoints and reduces the amplification of misinformation. Furthermore, supporting independent journalism and promoting fact-checking initiatives are essential for ensuring that accurate and reliable information is readily available. Ultimately, fostering a culture of critical thinking, open dialogue, and a commitment to truth is essential for mitigating the harmful effects of echo chambers and building a more informed and resilient society. The challenge lies in navigating the complexities of the digital age while preserving the principles of informed public discourse and a shared understanding of reality. Only through conscious effort and collaborative action can we hope to break free from the confines of echo chambers and foster a more informed and enlightened citizenry.

Let's analyze the psychological factors that make individuals susceptible to conspiracy theories and propaganda.

In an era defined by unprecedented access to information, paradoxically, the proliferation of misinformation has emerged as a significant societal challenge. This phenomenon, often fueled by the "echo chamber effect," highlights the dangers of self-selection and confirmation bias in the digital age. The echo chamber effect, characterized by individuals primarily encountering information that reinforces their existing beliefs, creates an environment where dissenting voices are marginalized and inaccurate narratives can flourish. Understanding the psychological factors that predispose individuals to conspiracy theories and propaganda is crucial to mitigating the detrimental impact of this trend.

The echo chamber effect is exacerbated by algorithmic curation, where social media platforms and search engines prioritize content based on user engagement and past behavior. This creates personalized information bubbles, limiting exposure to diverse perspectives and reinforcing pre-existing biases. Individuals are presented with a skewed reality, where their own beliefs appear to be the dominant viewpoint, leading to a false sense of consensus and further entrenching their convictions. This insular environment can then become fertile ground for the acceptance and spread of misinformation, including conspiracy theories and propaganda.

Several psychological factors contribute to the susceptibility of individuals to these harmful narratives. One of the most prominent is confirmation bias, the tendency to selectively seek out and interpret information that confirms pre-existing beliefs while ignoring or downplaying contradictory evidence. In an echo chamber, confirmation bias is amplified as individuals are primarily exposed to content that validates their worldview. This reinforcement loop strengthens their existing convictions, making them resistant to alternative perspectives, even when presented with credible evidence.

Furthermore, cognitive dissonance, the psychological discomfort experienced when holding conflicting beliefs, plays a crucial role. To alleviate this discomfort, individuals may actively dismiss or discredit information that challenges their worldview, further reinforcing their reliance on sources that align with their pre-existing beliefs. In the context of conspiracy theories, this can manifest as a rejection of mainstream media narratives in favor of alternative explanations that offer a simpler, albeit inaccurate, understanding of complex events.

Beyond confirmation bias and cognitive dissonance, social identity theory sheds light on how group affiliation influences susceptibility to misinformation. Individuals often derive a sense of belonging and self-worth from identifying with a particular group, whether it be a political party, a religious sect, or a community centered around a shared ideology. This strong group identity can lead to in-group bias, where members perceive their own group as superior and view out-groups with suspicion or hostility. Consequently, individuals may be more likely to accept information that reinforces the group's beliefs, even if it is demonstrably false, and reject information that challenges the group's narrative, regardless of its validity. The fear of social ostracization within the group further reinforces this tendency, as individuals may be reluctant to express dissenting opinions for fear of jeopardizing their social standing.

Another contributing factor is the need for closure, the desire for definite answers and certainty, particularly in times of uncertainty and anxiety. Conspiracy theories often offer seemingly simple explanations for complex events, providing a sense of control and understanding in a world that can feel chaotic and unpredictable. This can be particularly appealing to individuals who feel marginalized or disenfranchised, as conspiracy theories offer a narrative that empowers them by suggesting they possess secret knowledge that others are unaware of.

Additionally, the availability heuristic can contribute to the spread of misinformation. This cognitive bias involves estimating the likelihood of an event based on how easily examples of it come to mind. If individuals are repeatedly exposed to a particular narrative, even if it is false, they may overestimate its prevalence and accept it as true. The echo chamber effect exacerbates this bias by flooding individuals with repetitive and sensationalized content, making it more readily available in their minds and influencing their perceptions of reality.

Addressing the echo chamber effect and the spread of misinformation requires a multi-faceted approach. Promoting media literacy and critical thinking skills is essential to equipping individuals with the tools to evaluate information critically and identify potential biases. This includes teaching individuals how to identify credible sources, recognize manipulative techniques, and understand the difference between correlation and causation.

Platforms have a responsibility to mitigate the amplification of misinformation through algorithmic curation. This could involve prioritizing content from reputable sources, de-emphasizing engagement-based rankings, and implementing strategies to expose users to a wider range of perspectives. However, these efforts must be carefully balanced with the need to protect freedom of expression and avoid censorship.

Finally, fostering dialogue and empathy across ideological divides is crucial to breaking down echo chambers and promoting a more nuanced understanding of complex issues. This requires creating spaces where individuals can engage in respectful conversations with those who hold different beliefs, challenging their own assumptions, and recognizing the shared humanity that binds them together. Only through a collective effort can we hope to navigate the challenges of the information age and build a more informed and resilient society. The fight against misinformation is not just about debunking false claims; it's about fostering a culture of critical thinking, empathy, and intellectual humility, enabling individuals to navigate the complexities of the modern world with greater wisdom and discernment.

FROM PROTEST TO POLARIZATION
The Seeds of Division

Let's explore the increasing polarization of society along political, cultural, and ideological lines.

In contemporary society, a disquieting trend is taking hold: the increasing polarization of communities along political, cultural, and ideological lines. Once vibrant and diverse public spheres are fracturing into echo chambers, where individuals primarily interact with and reinforce their pre-existing beliefs. This essay will explore the multifaceted roots of this growing polarization, examining how legitimate protest can morph into entrenched division, hindering constructive dialogue and threatening the very fabric of social cohesion.

One of the primary catalysts for this polarization is the rise of identity politics. While movements centered on the rights and recognition of marginalized groups have undeniably achieved important progress, they have also inadvertently contributed to a heightened sense of group identity and, in some cases, a perception of inherent conflict between groups. When individuals primarily identify with a specific group (based on race, gender, sexual orientation, or other characteristics), it can become easier to view those outside that group as "other" – potentially leading to suspicion, animosity, and a zero-sum mentality where one group's gain is perceived as another's loss. This is not to diminish the importance of addressing historical injustices or advocating for equality, but rather to acknowledge the potential for unintended consequences when group identity becomes overly emphasized at the expense of shared values and common humanity.

The media landscape, particularly the advent of social media, has profoundly accelerated this trend. Algorithms designed to maximize engagement often prioritize sensational and emotionally charged content, which frequently reinforces existing biases and exposes individuals to increasingly extreme viewpoints. The filter bubble effect, where users are primarily exposed to information confirming their pre-existing beliefs, further entrenches these divisions. Furthermore, the anonymity afforded by online platforms can embolden individuals to engage in inflammatory rhetoric and personal attacks, further poisoning the public discourse. The traditional media, struggling to maintain relevance in this fragmented environment, can also fall prey to catering to specific ideological niches, further exacerbating polarization by presenting information through a partisan lens. The 24-hour news cycle, with its constant demand for fresh content, can also contribute to the problem by focusing on conflict and controversy, often at the expense of nuanced analysis and balanced reporting.

Economic inequality is another significant driver of polarization. The widening gap between the rich and the poor creates resentment and fuels a sense of injustice. Those who feel left behind by economic progress may be more susceptible to populist rhetoric that scapegoats specific groups or promotes simplistic solutions to complex problems. This economic anxiety can manifest as political anger, directed at elites, immigrants, or other perceived threats to their economic security. The decline of traditional industries and the rise of the gig economy have further contributed to economic insecurity, making individuals feel more vulnerable and less connected to traditional social safety nets, which can in turn fuel political instability and polarization.

Furthermore, a decline in civic education and critical thinking skills has left many individuals ill-equipped to navigate the complex information landscape and engage in reasoned debate. Without a solid understanding of history, civics, and logical reasoning, individuals are more likely to be swayed by misinformation, propaganda, and emotional appeals. This lack of critical thinking skills also makes it more difficult to engage in constructive dialogue with those who hold different viewpoints, as individuals may be unable to understand or appreciate alternative perspectives. The erosion of trust in institutions, including government, media, and academia, further exacerbates this problem, making it more difficult to find common ground and build consensus.

The consequences of this increasing polarization are far-reaching and potentially devastating. It hinders the ability to address critical societal challenges, such as climate change, healthcare reform, and economic inequality, as political gridlock and partisan bickering prevent meaningful progress. It erodes social trust and cohesion, making communities more fragmented and less resilient. It can also lead to political violence and instability, as individuals become increasingly willing to resort to extreme measures to defend their beliefs. In the long term, unchecked polarization threatens the very foundations of democratic governance by undermining the principles of compromise, consensus-building, and respect for dissenting opinions.

Speaking of this growing polarization requires a multi-faceted approach. First, it is crucial to promote media literacy and critical thinking skills, empowering individuals to evaluate information critically and resist manipulation. This requires investing in education and promoting access to diverse sources of information. Second, it is essential to foster dialogue and understanding across ideological divides.

This can be achieved through community-based initiatives, structured conversations, and online platforms designed to promote respectful engagement with opposing viewpoints. Third, it is vital to address the underlying economic anxieties that fuel polarization by promoting policies that reduce inequality and create economic opportunity for all. This includes investing in education, job training, and social safety nets. Finally, it is imperative to reform the media landscape to reduce the spread of misinformation and promote more balanced and nuanced reporting. This may require stricter regulations on social media platforms, increased funding for public broadcasting, and a renewed commitment to journalistic ethics.

The shift from protest to polarization represents a significant challenge to contemporary society. While protest is a vital mechanism for social change, unchecked polarization can undermine democratic institutions and erode social cohesion. By understanding the complex roots of this phenomenon and implementing effective strategies to promote dialogue, critical thinking, and economic justice, we can begin to bridge the divides that threaten to tear us apart and build a more inclusive and resilient society. The future of our communities, and indeed our democracy, depends on our ability to overcome this challenge and find common ground in a world increasingly defined by division.

Let's explore the impact of identity politics and the weaponization of social justice issues.

The 21st century has witnessed an explosion of activism and social movements, fueled by a desire for greater equality, justice, and representation. From the Occupy movement to Black Lives Matter, and the #MeToo movement, citizens have taken to the streets and the internet to demand systemic change. While these protests often originate from legitimate grievances and a pursuit of positive societal transformation, their evolution has, in many instances, contributed to a growing sense of polarization. This essay will examine how the rise of identity politics and the perceived weaponization of social justice issues have sown seeds of division, complicating the path towards a more unified and equitable future.

The rise of identity politics is a central factor in understanding contemporary polarization. Identity politics, in its essence, involves organizing and mobilizing around shared experiences and concerns related to aspects of one's identity, such as race, ethnicity, gender, sexual orientation, or religion. Proponents argue that identity politics is crucial for giving voice to marginalized groups, addressing historical injustices, and fostering a sense of belonging and empowerment. By highlighting the unique challenges faced by specific communities, identity politics can bring attention to systemic inequalities that might otherwise be ignored. For example, movements centered on racial justice have exposed the persistent impact of discriminatory practices in areas like policing, housing, and employment. Similarly, feminist movements have challenged patriarchal structures and advocated for gender equality in various spheres of life.

However, the emphasis on identity can also lead to unintended consequences. One potential pitfall is the creation of echo chambers, where individuals primarily interact with those who share their viewpoints, reinforcing existing beliefs and limiting exposure to alternative perspectives. This can lead to increased animosity towards those perceived as "other" or as belonging to opposing identity groups. Furthermore, an overemphasis on group identity can sometimes overshadow individual agency and complexity, leading to generalizations and stereotypes. Critics argue that identity politics can fragment society into competing factions, making it difficult to find common ground and build broad-based coalitions. There is a risk that focusing solely on group-specific grievances can detract from universal values and principles that could unite people across different backgrounds.

The term "weaponization of social justice issues" describes a phenomenon where concerns about fairness and equality are used strategically to gain political advantage, silence dissent, or demonize opponents. This can manifest in various ways, such as accusing individuals or organizations of bias or discrimination without sufficient evidence, or using social media campaigns to shame or ostracize those who express unpopular opinions. While genuine instances of injustice undoubtedly exist, the selective or exaggerated use of such accusations can erode trust in institutions, stifle open debate, and create a climate of fear.

One area where the weaponization of social justice issues is often observed is in online discourse. Social media platforms, while providing valuable tools for organizing and disseminating information, can also amplify outrage and facilitate the rapid spread of misinformation. The concept of "cancel culture," for instance, involves publicly shaming individuals for perceived transgressions, often leading to job losses or social isolation. While intended to hold people accountable for their actions, cancel culture can sometimes be disproportionate and unforgiving, punishing minor offenses with severe consequences. Moreover, the fear of being "canceled" can discourage people from expressing controversial or unpopular opinions, even if those opinions are based on legitimate concerns or good-faith arguments.

Another way in which social justice issues can be weaponized is through the manipulation of language and rhetoric. Terms like "woke" or "virtue signaling" are often used to criticize those who express support for progressive causes, implying that their motivations are insincere or that they are simply trying to gain social approval. This type of rhetoric can be used to dismiss legitimate concerns about inequality or injustice, and to create a false dichotomy between those who are genuinely committed to social change and those who are simply performative.

It is crucial to acknowledge that the line between genuine advocacy and the weaponization of social justice issues can be blurry. What one person perceives as a legitimate attempt to address inequality; another may see as an unfair attack or an attempt to silence opposing viewpoints. Navigating these complexities requires critical thinking, empathy, and a willingness to engage in respectful dialogue, even when disagreements are strong.

While the pursuit of social justice is a noble and necessary endeavor, the rise of identity politics and the perceived weaponization of social justice issues have contributed to a growing sense of polarization in contemporary society. By recognizing the potential pitfalls of these trends, fostering open and honest dialogue, and focusing on shared values and common goals, we can strive to bridge divides and build a more inclusive and equitable future for all. It requires a commitment to nuanced understanding, a willingness to listen to opposing viewpoints, and a rejection of simplistic narratives that perpetuate division. Ultimately, the path towards a more just society lies in finding ways to reconcile the particularity of identity with the universality of human rights and dignity.

Let's analyze the role of online activism and its potential for both positive change and division.

The digital age has fundamentally reshaped the landscape of social and political activism. Online platforms, once hailed as democratizing forces, have become both powerful tools for mobilization and potential breeding grounds for division. While offering unprecedented opportunities for collective action and amplified voices, the very architecture of online activism can inadvertently contribute to societal polarization, creating echo chambers and exacerbating existing fault lines. This essay will analyze the multifaceted role of online activism, exploring its potential for positive change while critically examining the mechanisms through which it can foster division and contribute to a more fragmented public sphere.

One of the most significant benefits of online activism is its ability to connect individuals across geographical boundaries, fostering a sense of shared purpose and facilitating rapid mobilization. Social media platforms like Twitter, Facebook, and Instagram have become instrumental in organizing protests, disseminating information, and raising awareness about critical social issues. The Arab Spring, for example, demonstrated the potent force of online activism in challenging authoritarian regimes and demanding democratic reforms. Similarly, the #BlackLivesMatter movement gained global momentum through viral videos, shared personal narratives, and coordinated online campaigns, prompting widespread conversations about racial injustice and police brutality. Online petitions, crowdfunding initiatives, and virtual town halls provide avenues for civic engagement that were previously inaccessible to many, empowering marginalized communities and enabling them to participate in democratic processes. The speed and scale at which online movements can gain traction offer a crucial counterweight to traditional power structures, holding institutions accountable and demanding social change with unprecedented urgency.

However, the very features that make online activism so effective can also contribute to its divisive potential. Algorithms designed to maximize user engagement often prioritize emotionally charged content, leading to the creation of echo chambers where individuals are primarily exposed to information that confirms their existing beliefs. This phenomenon, known as "filter bubbling," can reinforce pre-existing biases, limit exposure to diverse perspectives, and foster a sense of moral superiority among those who believe they are on the "right" side of an issue. Within these echo chambers, dissenting voices are often silenced or dismissed, leading to a decline in critical thinking and a reduced capacity for empathy and understanding. The anonymity afforded by online platforms can further exacerbate this problem, emboldening individuals to engage in aggressive or hateful rhetoric without fear of real-world consequences.

Furthermore, the performative nature of some online activism can contribute to a climate of division. The pressure to publicly signal one's commitment to a cause can lead to virtue signaling, where individuals prioritize outward displays of support over genuine engagement with the underlying issues. This can create a sense of competition and judgment within activist communities, with individuals policing each other's behavior and demanding adherence to increasingly rigid ideological standards. The fear of being "canceled" or publicly shamed for expressing unpopular opinions can stifle open dialogue and discourage nuanced debate, further entrenching polarized positions. The focus on online metrics – likes, shares, and retweets – can also incentivize sensationalism and outrage, rewarding content that provokes strong emotional reactions rather than promoting thoughtful analysis and constructive solutions.

Beyond the internal dynamics of online activist communities, the spread of misinformation and disinformation poses a significant threat to social cohesion. Malicious actors can exploit social media platforms to spread false narratives, sow discord, and manipulate public opinion. The proliferation of "fake news" and conspiracy theories can undermine trust in legitimate sources of information, making it increasingly difficult for individuals to discern fact from fiction. This erosion of trust can have profound consequences, fueling political polarization, eroding social capital, and even inciting violence. The Cambridge Analytica scandal, for example, demonstrated the potential for data mining and targeted advertising to be used to manipulate voters and influence election outcomes, highlighting the vulnerability of democratic processes to online manipulation.

Focusing on the challenges posed by online activism requires a multi-faceted approach. Media literacy education is crucial for equipping individuals with the skills to critically evaluate online information and identify misinformation. Social media platforms need to take greater responsibility for combating the spread of hate speech, disinformation, and manipulative content, while also protecting freedom of expression. Algorithmic transparency and greater user control over content feeds can help to break down echo chambers and promote exposure to diverse perspectives. Furthermore, fostering constructive dialogue and encouraging empathy across ideological divides is essential for bridging societal divides. This requires creating spaces for respectful conversation, promoting critical thinking, and challenging the tendency to demonize those with opposing viewpoints.

In conclusion, online activism presents a complex and paradoxical phenomenon. While offering unparalleled opportunities for social and political mobilization, it also carries the risk of exacerbating societal divisions and undermining democratic discourse. By understanding the mechanisms through which online platforms can contribute to polarization, and by taking proactive steps to promote media literacy, algorithmic transparency, and constructive dialogue, we can harness the power of online activism for positive change while mitigating its potential harms. The future of democracy may well depend on our ability to navigate the increasingly complex and contested digital landscape.

THE RISE OF THE STRONGMAN
Case Studies in Authoritarian Drift

The rise of strongman leaders across the globe in recent decades has prompted a renewed interest in understanding the archetype itself, dissecting its characteristics, and analyzing its impact on democratic institutions. While the term "strongman" might conjure images of brute force and overt dictatorship, the reality is far more nuanced. The strongman, as a political figure, thrives not solely on coercion but on a complex interplay of carefully cultivated personality, strategically deployed rhetoric, and a calculated disregard for the established norms of governance. This essay aims to define the strongman archetype by exploring the key characteristics that define these leaders, examining their methods of consolidating and maintaining power, and contextualizing their rule within the spectrum of authoritarianism.

One of the most recognizable hallmarks of a strongman leader is the cult of personality. This is not merely about popularity; it's a deliberate and meticulously constructed image of the leader as infallible, indispensable, and uniquely capable of leading the nation to greatness. The strongman actively cultivates this aura through carefully crafted appearances, staged events, and the pervasive promotion of their image in state-controlled media. They are often portrayed as figures of strength, decisiveness, and even near-mythical status, embodying the aspirations and perceived virtues of the nation. This deliberate creation of a larger-than-life persona serves several purposes. First, it fosters a sense of unwavering loyalty and obedience among the population. Second, it discourages dissent by making any criticism of the leader appear as an attack on the nation itself. Finally, it centralizes power in the hands of the individual, effectively blurring the lines between the leader and the state. Examples abound, from the carefully curated ruggedness of Vladimir Putin to the paternalistic pronouncements of Rodrigo Duterte, each leader employing distinct strategies to solidify their cult of personality.

Closely intertwined with the cult of personality is the deployment of nationalist rhetoric. The strongman typically positions themselves as the defender of the nation against internal and external threats, often exaggerating these dangers to justify their actions and consolidate support. This rhetoric frequently taps into existing feelings of national pride, historical grievances, and anxieties about cultural identity. They often present a romanticized vision of the nation's past and promise to restore its former glory, appealing to a sense of collective identity and purpose. This narrative often involves scapegoating minority groups, immigrants, or foreign powers as enemies of the nation, thus diverting attention from internal problems and consolidating support around the leader. The use of nationalist sentiment serves as a powerful tool for legitimizing their power and silencing opposition, as any criticism of the leader can be framed as an attack on national unity and sovereignty. The rise of right-wing populism in Europe and the Americas provides numerous examples of strongman leaders effectively utilizing nationalist rhetoric to gain and maintain power.

Underpinning the cult of personality and nationalist rhetoric is the systematic suppression of dissent. Strongman leaders often target independent media outlets, civil society organizations, and political opponents, employing a range of tactics to silence critical voices. This can include direct censorship, restrictive laws, strategic lawsuits, and even intimidation and violence. The suppression of dissent creates a climate of fear and self-censorship, discouraging any challenge to the leader's authority. By controlling the flow of information and silencing alternative perspectives, the strongman can maintain their grip on power and prevent the emergence of organized opposition. This suppression isn't always explicit; often, it manifests as a gradual erosion of democratic norms and institutions, making it difficult for opposition voices to effectively challenge the ruling power.

Furthermore, strongman leaders exhibit a palpable disregard for the rule of law. They often manipulate legal systems to serve their own interests, undermining judicial independence and selectively enforcing laws against their opponents. This disregard for the rule of law erodes public trust in institutions and creates a climate of impunity, allowing the strongman and their allies to operate above the law. They may appoint loyalists to key positions in the judiciary, manipulate electoral processes, and even rewrite constitutions to consolidate their power. This erosion of legal frameworks is a critical step in the transition from a functioning democracy to an authoritarian state, as it removes the safeguards that are designed to protect individual rights and limit the power of the government.

Finally, the strongman relies heavily on propaganda and misinformation. This involves the deliberate dissemination of false or misleading information through state-controlled media, social media, and other channels. Propaganda aims to manipulate public opinion, reinforce the leader's narrative, and discredit opponents. Misinformation, often spread through online bots and fake news websites, can sow confusion, undermine trust in legitimate news sources, and erode public discourse. By controlling the narrative and shaping public perceptions, the strongman can maintain their grip on power and suppress any challenge to their authority. This manipulation of information is often sophisticated, employing psychological techniques to target specific audiences and exploit existing biases.

It's crucial to understand the distinction between authoritarianism and totalitarianism when analyzing strongman leaders. While both regimes involve the concentration of power in the hands of a single leader or a small group, totalitarianism represents a more complete and pervasive form of control. Totalitarian regimes seek to control every aspect of human life, from political and economic activity to personal beliefs and cultural expression. Authoritarian regimes, on the other hand, typically focus on suppressing political opposition and maintaining order, but they may allow for some degree of individual freedom and economic activity. The strongman often occupies a gray area between these two extremes. While they may not seek to control every aspect of life, they actively suppress political dissent, manipulate the legal system, and control the flow of information, pushing their regimes closer to the authoritarian end of the spectrum. This ambiguity can make it difficult to classify strongman regimes definitively, but it also highlights the dangers they pose to democratic institutions and individual freedoms.

The strongman archetype is characterized by a complex interplay of personality, rhetoric, and tactics aimed at consolidating and maintaining power. The cult of personality, nationalist rhetoric, suppression of dissent, disregard for the rule of law, and use of propaganda and misinformation are all key elements of this archetype. While strongman leaders often operate within a gray area between authoritarianism and totalitarianism, their actions invariably erode democratic institutions and undermine individual freedoms. Understanding the characteristics and methods of the strongman is therefore essential for defending democracy and resisting the rise of authoritarianism in the 21st century. By recognizing the warning signs and proactively addressing the underlying causes that contribute to the rise of these figures, societies can work to strengthen democratic institutions and prevent the erosion of fundamental rights and freedoms.

The Enduring Allure and Peril *of the* Strongman

The specter of the strongman looms large throughout history, a recurring figure whose iron grip has shaped nations and defined eras. From the ancient emperors who commanded absolute obedience to the 20th-century dictators who plunged the world into war, the charismatic leader who promises order and decisive action in times of chaos has held an enduring, if perilous, allure. Understanding the historical context of these figures – the recurring patterns in their strategies, the conditions that paved their path to power, and the enduring legacy of colonialism – is crucial to recognizing and resisting the resurgence of authoritarian tendencies in the modern world.

Looking back, figures like Benito Mussolini in Italy, Francisco Franco in Spain, and Juan Perón in Argentina offer stark examples of the strongman archetype. Mussolini, leveraging the post-World War I disillusionment and fear of communist revolution, cultivated a personality cult and promised a return to Roman glory. Franco, seizing power after a bloody civil war, established a repressive regime that prioritized national unity and suppressed dissent. Perón, appealing to the working class with populist policies and nationalist rhetoric, built a formidable power base that challenged the established elite. While their ideologies and specific contexts differed, these leaders shared a common playbook, a recurring pattern of tactics designed to consolidate power and suppress opposition.

One prevalent tactic was the manipulation of national identity and historical narratives. Strongmen often present themselves as saviors, uniquely qualified to restore their nation to a perceived golden age. They rewrite history, selectively highlighting events to reinforce their narrative of national greatness and demonize perceived enemies, both internal and external. This manipulation of collective memory serves to legitimize their rule and foster a sense of national unity under their leadership. Mussolini's invocation of the Roman Empire, Franco's defense of traditional Spanish values against "godless communism," and Perón's championing of Argentine sovereignty against foreign influence all exemplify this strategy.

Another common thread is the cultivation of a personality cult. Strongmen project an image of strength, decisiveness, and infallibility, often through propaganda and the manipulation of media. They control the narrative, suppressing any dissenting voices and promoting a carefully crafted image of themselves as the sole protectors of the nation. This personality cult instills a sense of loyalty and obedience among the populace, making it more difficult to challenge their authority. The omnipresent imagery and slogans associated with these leaders, from

Mussolini's "Il Duce" to Franco's "Caudillo," served to reinforce their dominance and suppress any alternative narratives.

The suppression of political opposition is a hallmark of strongman rule. This often involves the use of violence, intimidation, and censorship to silence critics and dismantle democratic institutions. Political parties are banned or co-opted, elections are rigged, and independent media outlets are shut down. The rule of law is undermined, and the judiciary is brought under the control of the executive branch, effectively dismantling any checks and balances on the leader's power. The brutal repression employed by Mussolini's fascist squads, Franco's Falangist forces, and Perón's security apparatus demonstrates the willingness of strongmen to use force to maintain their grip on power.

These figures rarely rise to power in a vacuum. Their emergence is typically facilitated by a confluence of historical conditions that create fertile ground for authoritarianism. Economic depression, political instability, and social unrest often leave populations feeling vulnerable and disillusioned with existing institutions. The promise of a strong leader who can restore order and stability can be particularly appealing in such circumstances. The widespread economic hardship and political fragmentation that followed World War I in Europe, for instance, created an environment ripe for the rise of figures like Mussolini. Similarly, the deep social divisions and political polarization that plagued Spain in the 1930s paved the way for Franco's ascent.

Beyond immediate crises, the legacy of colonialism also plays a significant role in shaping post-colonial states susceptible to strongman rule. Colonial powers often left behind weak institutions, arbitrary borders, and deep-seated social inequalities. The disruption of traditional social structures and the imposition of foreign political systems created power vacuums that aspiring strongmen were quick to exploit. The artificial nature of many post-colonial states, lacking a strong sense of national identity, made them vulnerable to divisive rhetoric and the appeal of a unifying, authoritarian figure. The wave of military coups and authoritarian regimes that swept across Africa and Latin America in the decades following independence underscores the enduring impact of colonialism on the political landscape of these regions.

The historical context of strongman rule reveals alarming patterns: the manipulation of national identity, the cultivation of personality cults, the suppression of opposition, and the exploitation of societal vulnerabilities. By understanding these recurring themes, we can better recognize the warning signs of authoritarianism and resist the seductive appeal of the strongman's promise of order and stability. A critical examination of history serves as a vital safeguard against repeating the mistakes of the past, reminding us that the pursuit of genuine democracy, respect for human rights, and the rule of law are essential to preventing the rise of future strongmen and safeguarding the freedoms that they invariably seek to suppress. Embracing a nuanced understanding of the past is not just an academic exercise, but a crucial act of vigilance in preserving a future where the echoes of authoritarianism are finally silenced.

A CASE STUDY
VLADIMIR PUTIN'S RUSSIA

Vladimir Putin's rise to power in Russia and his subsequent consolidation of authority offers a compelling case study in authoritarian governance in the 21st century. From a relatively unknown figure within the Kremlin to the dominant force in Russian politics, Putin's journey has been marked by a calculated and multifaceted approach to controlling the narrative, suppressing dissent, and projecting Russian strength on the global stage. This essay will analyze the key elements of Putin's ascent and tenure, examining the methods employed to consolidate power, the devastating impact on Russian civil society and political institutions, and the far-reaching implications for international relations.

Putin's ascent to the presidency in 1999 was facilitated by a confluence of factors. The waning popularity of Boris Yeltsin, plagued by health problems and accusations of corruption, created a power vacuum. Putin, as the relatively new and assertive head of the FSB (Federal Security Service), was strategically positioned to capitalize on this instability. His background in the security services resonated with a public yearning for order and stability after the turbulent years of post-Soviet transition. The Second Chechen War, initiated shortly before Yeltsin's resignation, provided a crucial opportunity for Putin to project an image of decisive leadership and national strength. He successfully framed the conflict as a fight against terrorism and for the territorial integrity of Russia, bolstering public support and establishing himself as a strong and reliable figure capable of defending national interests.

Once in power, Putin systematically implemented strategies to solidify his control over the Russian political landscape. A key element of this strategy was the **control of the media**. Independent media outlets, which had flourished in the Yeltsin era, were systematically brought under state control or forced into self-censorship. Prominent independent television channels like NTV were acquired by state-owned entities or individuals loyal to the Kremlin, effectively silencing critical voices and shaping the public narrative in favor of the government. Journalists who dared to investigate corruption or criticize the regime faced harassment, intimidation, and even violence, creating a climate of fear that stifled independent reporting. This control over the media allowed the Kremlin to control the flow of information, manipulate public opinion, and project a carefully cultivated image of Putin as a strong, competent, and patriotic leader.

Another critical aspect of Putin's consolidation of power was the **suppression of opposition**. Political opponents, particularly those with genuine popular support, faced a range of tactics designed to marginalize and silence them. Registration requirements for political parties were tightened, making it difficult for new or independent parties to participate in elections. Leading opposition figures like Mikhail Khodorkovsky were targeted with politically motivated prosecutions, effectively removing them from the political arena. Protests and demonstrations were often met with heavy-handed police tactics, and organizers faced arrest and prosecution. This systematic suppression of dissent created a climate of fear and discouraged open political debate, effectively silencing alternative voices and consolidating the dominant position of the ruling United Russia party.

Furthermore, Putin skillfully **cultivated nationalist sentiment** to bolster his legitimacy and consolidate his support base. He frequently invoked Russia's historical greatness, emphasizing its unique civilization and its rightful place as a major world power. He portrayed the West as a hostile force seeking to undermine Russia's sovereignty and influence, tapping into deep-seated anxieties and historical grievances. By appealing to patriotic sentiments and promoting a sense of national unity, Putin successfully mobilized popular support and deflected criticism of his domestic policies. This cultivation of nationalist sentiment also served to legitimize his assertive foreign policy agenda, positioning Russia as a defender of its national interests and a counterweight to Western dominance.

Complementary to this was the systematic **use of disinformation and propaganda**, both domestically and internationally. Domestically, state-controlled media outlets disseminated a consistent message that glorified Putin, demonized his opponents, and downplayed or ignored problems facing the country. Internationally, Russia launched sophisticated disinformation campaigns aimed at influencing public opinion in other countries, undermining trust in democratic institutions, and sowing discord. These campaigns often involved the use of social media, troll farms, and state-sponsored media outlets to spread false or misleading information, often exploiting existing social divisions and anxieties. The goal was to undermine the credibility of Western narratives and promote a Russian perspective on global events.

The integrity of the electoral process also suffered under Putin's rule, with allegations of **manipulation of elections** becoming commonplace. Measures were taken to ensure the dominance of the ruling United Russia party, including biased media coverage, restrictions on opposition campaigning, and allegations of vote rigging. International observers frequently criticized the Russian electoral process for failing to meet international standards of fairness and transparency. By manipulating elections, Putin ensured that the ruling party maintained its dominance in parliament, providing a veneer of legitimacy for his policies and further consolidating his control over the political system.

The impact of Putin's consolidation of power on **Russian civil society and political institutions** has been profound and detrimental. Independent civil society organizations, including human rights groups, environmental organizations, and independent media outlets, have faced increasing pressure and restrictions. Legislation was enacted to label organizations receiving foreign funding as "foreign agents," stigmatizing them and hindering their ability to operate effectively. The space for independent political activity has shrunk dramatically, with dissent increasingly silenced and opposition parties marginalized. The judicial system, once envisioned as a safeguard against arbitrary state power, has become increasingly subservient to the executive branch, undermining the rule of law and further eroding checks and balances.

Finally, Putin's domestic policies have been mirrored by an **assertive foreign policy** marked by interventions in neighboring countries. The 2008 war with Georgia and the 2014 annexation of Crimea, followed by the ongoing conflict in eastern Ukraine, demonstrated Putin's willingness to use military force to protect perceived Russian interests and challenge the existing international order. These interventions have been accompanied by aggressive rhetoric and accusations of Western interference in Russia's sphere of influence. Putin's foreign policy has been characterized by a desire to restore Russia's great power status, challenge what he sees as Western hegemony, and protect the interests of Russian-speaking populations in neighboring countries. This assertive foreign policy has led to increased tensions with the West and has contributed to a deterioration of international security.

Vladimir Putin's rise to power and subsequent consolidation of authority provides a stark illustration of how a determined leader can manipulate democratic institutions, suppress dissent, and exploit nationalist sentiment to establish and maintain authoritarian rule. His control of the media, suppression of opposition, cultivation of nationalist sentiment, use of disinformation and propaganda, and manipulation of elections have had a devastating impact on Russian civil society and political institutions. Furthermore, his assertive foreign policy has destabilized the region and challenged the international order. Understanding the methods and consequences of Putin's rule is crucial for comprehending the current state of Russian politics and for developing effective strategies to promote democracy and human rights in the region. The long-term consequences of Putin's legacy remain to be seen, but it is clear that his actions have profoundly shaped the political landscape of Russia and its relationship with the rest of the world.

Underlying Factors Contributing to the Rise of Strongmen

The resurgence of strongman rule in various parts of the world is a concerning trend, threatening the foundations of democratic governance and international stability. While each instance of authoritarian consolidation is unique and shaped by specific local conditions, certain underlying factors consistently contribute to the rise of these figures. Examining these factors – economic anxieties, cultural grievances, weakened civil society, the role of social media and disinformation, and the erosion of democratic norms and institutions – provides a crucial framework for understanding and combatting this global phenomenon.

Economic Anxieties: Fueling the Populist Fire

Economic hardship and insecurity are fertile ground for the seeds of authoritarianism. The accelerating forces of globalization, while bringing overall economic growth, have also created winners and losers. For many, the promised benefits have failed to materialize, leading to widespread anxieties about job security, wage stagnation, and the erosion of national sovereignty. The integration of national economies into a global marketplace has often resulted in the outsourcing of jobs to countries with lower labor costs, leaving many feeling disenfranchised and vulnerable. This displacement, coupled with the inherent risks of global economic fluctuations, contributes to a pervasive sense of instability.

The stark reality of rising inequality exacerbates these anxieties. The concentration of wealth in the hands of a few, fueled by factors like technological advancements favoring skilled labor and the decline of organized labor movements, creates resentment and a sense of injustice. The perception that the system is rigged in favor of elites becomes a potent narrative exploited by aspiring strongmen. They often capitalize on this frustration by promising quick fixes and populist solutions, such as protectionist policies, nationalization of industries, and direct cash transfers, all designed to appeal to the immediate needs and anxieties of the economically vulnerable. These promises, though often unsustainable or ultimately detrimental, resonate deeply with those struggling to make ends meet, providing a powerful platform for the consolidation of power. The allure of a strong leader who can "fix" the economy and protect "the people" from the perceived ravages of globalization is a siren song that proves increasingly difficult to resist in times of economic hardship.

Cultural Grievances: Exploiting Identity and Division

Beyond economic concerns, cultural grievances play a significant role in the rise of strongmen. Globalization, alongside its economic impact, has also led to a perceived cultural homogenization, threatening traditional values and local identities. This often manifests as resentment towards Western cultural influence and a yearning for a return to a perceived "golden age" of national identity. The rise of nationalism and identity politics, often fueled by ethno-religious divisions, is a direct consequence of this cultural anxiety.

Strongmen expertly exploit these pre-existing divisions, often constructing narratives that demonize minority groups, immigrants, or perceived "enemies" of the nation. They portray themselves as the defenders of national culture and tradition against these external threats, promising to restore national pride and protect the "true" identity of the people. This strategy often involves the manipulation of historical narratives, the selective interpretation of cultural symbols, and the scapegoating of marginalized communities. The demonization of "the other" serves to unite support behind the strongman's agenda, diverting attention from underlying economic and political problems. Religious and cultural institutions can be particularly susceptible to manipulation in this context, with strongmen often forging close alliances with religious leaders to legitimize their rule and rally support from religiously conservative segments of the population.

Weakened Civil Society: The Erosion of Resistance

A vibrant and active civil society is a crucial bulwark against authoritarianism. However, when trust in traditional institutions like political parties, independent media, and non-governmental organizations declines, the space for dissent and accountability shrinks, creating an environment ripe for the rise of strongmen. This decline in trust often stems from perceptions of corruption, inefficiency, and a disconnect between the ruling elite and the concerns of ordinary citizens.

Polarization and fragmentation of public discourse further weaken civil society. The increasing prevalence of echo chambers and filter bubbles online reinforces existing biases and makes it difficult to engage in constructive dialogue across ideological divides. This fragmentation makes it harder to build broad-based coalitions to resist authoritarian tendencies. Furthermore, strongmen often actively undermine civil society through restrictions on freedom of assembly and expression, curtailing the ability of opposition groups to organize and mobilize. Laws targeting NGOs, restrictions on media freedom, and the suppression of dissent through intimidation and violence are common tactics used to silence critical voices and consolidate power. The weakening of civil society leaves a vacuum that strongmen are eager to fill, further solidifying their grip on power.

THE ROLE OF SOCIAL MEDIA AND DISINFORMATION
Amplifying the Authoritarian Message

The advent of social media has profoundly altered the landscape of political communication, providing both opportunities and challenges for democratic governance. While social media can facilitate citizen engagement and promote transparency, it also presents a powerful tool for the spread of disinformation and the manipulation of public opinion. Strongmen have increasingly exploited these vulnerabilities to advance their agendas and consolidate their power.

The proliferation of fake news and propaganda on social media platforms erodes trust in traditional media outlets and creates confusion about facts and reality. This environment of uncertainty allows strongmen to control the narrative and shape public perception to their advantage. The creation of echo chambers and filter bubbles on social media platforms further exacerbates this problem, as individuals are primarily exposed to information that confirms their existing biases. This echo chamber effect reinforces extremist views and makes it more difficult to engage in reasoned debate. Furthermore, social media algorithms can be manipulated to amplify the reach of disinformation campaigns, ensuring that these messages reach a wider audience. The use of bots and fake accounts to spread propaganda and harass opposition voices is another tactic employed by strongmen to control the online narrative and silence dissent. The ability to directly communicate with citizens through social media, bypassing traditional media gatekeepers, allows strongmen to cultivate a personal following and circumvent scrutiny.

Erosion of Democratic Norms and Institutions: The Final Blow

Ultimately, the rise of strongmen is predicated on the erosion of democratic norms and institutions. A decline in political participation and civic engagement weakens the foundations of representative government, creating an opportunity for authoritarian forces to seize power. When citizens become disillusioned with the political process and lose faith in the ability of their elected representatives to address their concerns, they may be more susceptible to the appeal of a strong leader who promises to cut through the red tape and deliver results.

The weakening of checks and balances is another critical factor. When the executive branch becomes too powerful and the legislative and judicial branches are unable to effectively hold it accountable, it creates an environment where abuses of power can flourish. Strongmen often seek to undermine the independence of the judiciary, weaken the powers of parliament, and centralize authority in their own hands. Corruption and impunity further erode democratic norms and institutions. When public officials are perceived to be corrupt and unaccountable, it undermines public trust in the government and creates a sense of injustice. Strongmen often exploit this perception by promising to crack down on corruption, but in reality, they often use this rhetoric to consolidate their own power and enrich their allies. The gradual dismantling of democratic institutions, coupled with the erosion of democratic norms, creates a fertile ground for the rise of authoritarianism.

In conclusion, the rise of strongmen is a complex phenomenon driven by a confluence of interconnected factors. Economic anxieties, cultural grievances, weakened civil society, the manipulation of social media and disinformation, and the erosion of democratic norms and institutions all contribute to this disturbing trend. Addressing this challenge requires a multi-faceted approach that tackles these underlying causes. This includes promoting inclusive economic growth, fostering social cohesion and respect for diversity, strengthening civil society and independent media, combating disinformation, and reinforcing democratic institutions and the rule of law. Only by addressing these fundamental issues can we hope to reverse the tide of authoritarianism and safeguard the future of democracy.

Consequences of Authoritarian Drift

Authoritarian drift, the gradual erosion of democratic norms and institutions towards more autocratic governance, is a phenomenon with profound and far-reaching consequences. It is not a singular event, but rather a process that slowly chips away at the cornerstones of a free and just society, leading to a cascade of negative outcomes that impact human rights, economic stability, geopolitical relations, and ultimately, the global landscape of democratic values. The allure of strong leadership, often promising stability and order, can mask the insidious nature of this drift, making it all the more dangerous. Let's delve deeper into the specific consequences of this perilous shift.

HUMAN RIGHTS ABUSES
A Dark Stain
on Authoritarian Regimes

Perhaps the most visible and morally reprehensible consequence of authoritarian drift is the systematic abuse of human rights. The very foundation of a democratic society rests on the protection of individual liberties, including freedom of expression, assembly, and the pursuit of justice. As a government slides towards authoritarianism, these rights are invariably the first to be compromised.

- ## Suppression of Dissent and Freedom of Expression:

  Authoritarian regimes thrive on control, and silencing dissenting voices is paramount to maintaining their grip on power. This suppression manifests in various forms, from censorship of media outlets and online platforms to the banning of public gatherings and protests. Journalists, activists, and ordinary citizens who dare to criticize the government face intimidation, harassment, and legal persecution. The internet, once hailed as a tool for democratization, is increasingly weaponized for surveillance and the spread of propaganda, further limiting access to accurate information and stifling critical thought.

- ## Political Imprisonment and Torture:

  Opposition leaders, human rights defenders, and anyone perceived as a threat to the regime are often arbitrarily arrested and imprisoned on fabricated charges. The conditions in these prisons are frequently deplorable, with reports of overcrowding, inadequate sanitation, and denial of medical care being commonplace. Even more horrifying is the widespread use of torture and other forms of cruel, inhuman, and degrading treatment to extract confessions, punish dissent, and instill fear in the population. These acts represent a blatant disregard for human dignity and fundamental legal principles.

- **Discrimination Against Minorities:**

Authoritarian regimes often exploit existing societal divisions to consolidate their power. Minorities, whether based on ethnicity, religion, sexual orientation, or other characteristics, are frequently scapegoated and subjected to systematic discrimination. This can take the form of legal discrimination, such as discriminatory laws and policies, or social discrimination, such as hate speech and violence. In extreme cases, this can escalate to ethnic cleansing or even genocide, as witnessed in some of the most horrific events in human history.

ECONOMIC INSTABILITY:
The Rotten Fruit of Autocracy

While authoritarian leaders often promise economic prosperity and stability, the reality is that authoritarian drift inevitably leads to economic instability and decline. The lack of accountability, transparency, and the rule of law create an environment ripe for corruption and mismanagement, hindering economic growth and exacerbating inequality.

- **Corruption and Mismanagement:** In the absence of independent institutions and a free press, corruption flourishes under authoritarian rule. Government officials can engage in embezzlement, bribery, and other forms of corruption with impunity, diverting public funds for personal gain and enriching themselves at the expense of the people. This mismanagement extends to the economy as a whole, with resources being allocated inefficiently and projects being undertaken based on political considerations rather than economic merit.

- **Decline in Foreign Investment:** Foreign investors are wary of investing in countries with weak rule of law and a high risk of political instability. Authoritarian regimes often create an unpredictable and opaque business environment, discouraging foreign investment and hindering economic growth. The lack of protection for property rights and the risk of arbitrary government intervention further dampen investor confidence.

- **Increased Inequality:** The concentration of power and wealth in the hands of a small elite is a hallmark of authoritarian regimes. Cronyism and nepotism are rampant, with government contracts and other economic opportunities being awarded to those loyal to the regime. This leads to a widening gap between the rich and the poor, creating social unrest and fueling resentment towards the government.

GEOPOLITICAL INSTABILITY:
A Threat to Global Peace and Security

Authoritarian drift does not only impact the internal affairs of a nation; it also has significant implications for international relations and global stability. Authoritarian regimes are often more aggressive and unpredictable in their foreign policy, posing a threat to regional and global peace.

- ## Aggressive Foreign Policy and Military Interventions:

  Lacking domestic accountability, authoritarian leaders are often more willing to pursue aggressive foreign policies, including military interventions and territorial expansion. They may seek to distract from domestic problems by projecting power abroad or to rally nationalistic sentiment through confrontation with other countries. This can lead to armed conflicts, regional instability, and humanitarian crises.

- ## Strained Relations with International Allies:

  Authoritarian regimes often clash with democracies and international organizations over human rights, rule of law, and other fundamental values. This can lead to strained relations with international allies, isolation on the world stage, and difficulty in accessing international aid and support. The erosion of trust and cooperation between nations undermines global efforts to address shared challenges such as climate change, pandemics, and terrorism.

- ## Undermining of International Norms and Institutions:

  Authoritarian regimes often seek to undermine international norms and institutions that promote democracy, human rights, and the rule of law. They may refuse to comply with international treaties, challenge the authority of international courts, and support authoritarian governments in other countries. This can weaken the international system and make it more difficult to address global challenges.

DECLINE IN DEMOCRATIC VALUES GLOBALLY
A Contagion of Authoritarianism

Perhaps the most insidious consequence of authoritarian drift is its potential to undermine democratic values globally. The rise of authoritarian leaders and the success of authoritarian regimes can have a "demonstration effect," inspiring other would-be strongmen to emulate their tactics and pursue their own authoritarian ambitions.

- ## The "Demonstration Effect" of Successful Strongman Leaders:

  The perceived success of authoritarian regimes in achieving economic growth, maintaining social order, or projecting military power can make authoritarianism seem like an appealing alternative to democracy, particularly in countries struggling with political instability, economic challenges, or social divisions. This "demonstration effect" can embolden authoritarian leaders and weaken the resolve of democratic reformers.

- ## The Spread of Authoritarian Ideas and Practices:

  Authoritarian regimes actively promote their ideology and practices, often through propaganda, disinformation campaigns, and support for authoritarian movements in other countries. This can lead to the spread of authoritarian ideas and practices, such as censorship, surveillance, and the suppression of dissent, even in countries that are nominally democratic. This gradual erosion of democratic norms and institutions can ultimately pave the way for authoritarian drift.

The consequences of authoritarian drift are devastating and far-reaching, impacting human rights, economic stability, geopolitical relations, and the global landscape of democratic values. It is a process that must be resisted at every turn, both within individual nations and on the international stage. Strengthening democratic institutions, promoting the rule of law, protecting human rights, and fostering a vibrant civil society are essential to preventing authoritarian drift and safeguarding the future of democracy. Failure to do so risks plunging the world into a darker and more dangerous era, where individual liberties are suppressed, economic disparities widen, and global peace is threatened. The fight for democracy is a constant one, demanding vigilance and unwavering commitment to its principles.

THE NATIONALIST NARRATIVE
Rewriting History
and Silencing Dissent

Let's analyze how authoritarian regimes use nationalist narratives to consolidate power and suppress dissent.

Authoritarian regimes, in their pursuit of power and control, frequently employ a potent tool: the manipulation of history through nationalist narratives. These narratives, carefully crafted and relentlessly propagated, serve to consolidate power, legitimize the regime's actions, and, perhaps most importantly, silence dissent. By constructing a glorified past, emphasizing national unity, and demonizing external enemies, these regimes create an environment where questioning the status quo becomes tantamount to betraying the nation itself. This essay will examine how authoritarian regimes utilize nationalist narratives to achieve these goals, exploring the mechanisms of historical revisionism, the suppression of alternative viewpoints, and the chilling effect on intellectual freedom that results.

At the heart of the nationalist narrative lies the deliberate rewriting of history. This is not merely a matter of biased interpretation; it often involves the outright fabrication of events, the selective highlighting of certain figures and eras, and the suppression or distortion of inconvenient truths. This process aims to create a sanitized and idealized version of the national past, one that reinforces the regime's legitimacy and fosters a sense of national superiority. For instance, historical figures who challenged authority or championed unpopular causes are often demonized or erased from the historical record, while those who served the ruling ideology are elevated to near-mythical status. Battles are recounted with exaggerated displays of heroism, national achievements are magnified, and past wrongs committed by the nation are either justified or conveniently forgotten. This selective memory serves to cultivate a sense of collective pride and shared destiny, effectively binding the population to the regime's agenda.

Furthermore, nationalist narratives often rely on the construction of a monolithic national identity, often at the expense of acknowledging the diversity and complexity of the population. Ethnic minorities, religious groups, and regional identities that do not conform to the dominant narrative are often marginalized or actively repressed. The narrative frequently promotes the idea of a shared bloodline, common culture, and unified purpose, fostering a sense of "us" versus "them." This process of "othering" is crucial for mobilizing support against perceived enemies, both internal and external. By portraying dissenting voices as threats to national unity and security, regimes can justify the suppression of opposition and the implementation of draconian measures.

The control of information is paramount to the success of the nationalist narrative. Authoritarian regimes typically exert strict control over the media, education system, and cultural institutions, ensuring that the official historical narrative is disseminated widely and consistently.

Textbooks are rewritten to reflect the regime's ideology, independent media outlets are shut down, and dissenting voices are silenced through censorship, intimidation, and even imprisonment. The internet, a powerful tool for information sharing and independent thought, is often heavily censored, with access to alternative viewpoints restricted. Through this comprehensive control over information, the regime creates an echo chamber where the nationalist narrative is constantly reinforced, making it difficult for citizens to access alternative perspectives or challenge the official line.

The suppression of dissenting voices is not limited to the media and educational institutions. Intellectuals, artists, and academics who dare to question the official narrative are often targeted with harassment, persecution, and professional ostracization. Their work is often banned, their reputations smeared, and their livelihoods threatened. The fear of reprisal can create a climate of self-censorship, where individuals are afraid to express their true opinions for fear of the consequences. This chilling effect on intellectual freedom stifles creativity, inhibits critical thinking, and ultimately undermines the very foundations of a healthy and vibrant society.

Authoritarian regimes frequently use nationalist narratives to justify aggressive foreign policies and expansionist ambitions. By portraying neighboring countries as historical enemies or threats to national security, they can mobilize popular support for military intervention and territorial expansion. The narrative often emphasizes past grievances, historical claims, and the need to "protect" ethnic kin living in neighboring countries. This manipulation of history can be a potent tool for inciting nationalistic fervor and justifying actions that would otherwise be condemned by the international community.

However, the power of the nationalist narrative is not absolute. Despite the best efforts of authoritarian regimes, alternative narratives often persist within society, transmitted through oral traditions, underground publications, and the memories of those who lived through periods of repression. These alternative narratives can serve as a source of resistance and inspiration for those who seek to challenge the regime's control over history. Furthermore, access to information through the internet, despite censorship efforts, can provide citizens with alternative perspectives and expose the lies and distortions of the official narrative.

The manipulation of history through nationalist narratives is a powerful tool used by authoritarian regimes to consolidate power, silence dissent, and justify their actions. By rewriting the past, constructing a monolithic national identity, and suppressing alternative viewpoints, these regimes create an environment where questioning the status quo becomes a dangerous act of betrayal. However, the persistence of alternative narratives and the increasing availability of information through independent channels offer hope for challenging these narratives and fostering a more critical and nuanced understanding of history. Ultimately, the fight against the manipulation of history is a fight for truth, justice, and freedom of expression. It is a fight that must be waged to ensure that the past is not used to oppress the present and undermine the future.

A DANGEROUS MANIPULATION OF HISTORY
The Demonization of Minorities, and the Suppression of Opposition

In recent years, there has been a troubling trend of nationalistic narratives emerging around the world. These narratives often involve the manipulation of history, the demonization of minorities, and the suppression of opposition. This essay will explore these tactics in-depth and explain why they are so dangerous.

At the heart of the nationalist narrative is the manipulation of history. Nationalists often rewrite history to create a mythical past in which their nation was always great and powerful. They exaggerate the achievements of their ancestors and downplay or even deny any negative events or actions. This revisionist approach to history is not only intellectually dishonest, but it also has the potential to create a false sense of superiority among the nation's populace. This can lead to a dangerous "us versus them" mentality, in which the nation sees itself as inherently better than others.

Another tactic used by nationalists is the demonization of minorities. Nationalists often scapegoat minorities for society's problems, blaming them for everything from economic downturns to cultural decay. This can take the form of outright racism, Islamophobia, or other forms of bigotry. By creating a narrative in which minorities are to blame for society's ills, nationalists can rally their supporters around a common enemy and distract them from the real issues at hand.

Finally, nationalists often suppress opposition to their narrative. This can take many forms, from censorship and propaganda to outright violence. Nationalists seek to silence any voices that challenge their narrative or offer a different perspective. They do this to maintain their power and control over the narrative, and to prevent their supporters from being exposed to opposing viewpoints.

The nationalist narrative is a dangerous manipulation of history, the demonization of minorities, and the suppression of opposition. It is a tactic used by authoritarian regimes and extremist groups to maintain power and control over a population. It is a threat to democracy, freedom, and human rights. It is essential that we as a society recognize the dangers of the nationalist narrative and work to combat it through education, open dialogue, and the protection of democratic institutions.

Moreover, the nationalist narrative can be particularly appealing to certain groups of people who feel marginalized, disenfranchised or left behind by globalization, technological advancement and societal changes. Nationalistic leaders and parties often tap into these feelings and blame the "others" for these groups' struggles. This is a dangerous and short-sighted approach, as it fails to address the root causes of these struggles and only serves to further divide society.

Furthermore, the nationalist narrative often goes hand in hand with a lack of critical thinking and an over-reliance on emotions. Nationalistic leaders and parties often present their narrative in simple, black and white terms, and appeal to their supporters' emotions rather than their reason. This can be particularly effective in times of crisis, when people are looking for simple answers and someone to blame. However, it is a dangerous approach, as it leads to oversimplification of complex issues and can result in poor decision-making and policies.

In conclusion, the nationalist narrative is a dangerous manipulation of history, the demonization of minorities, and the suppression of opposition. It is a tactic used by authoritarian regimes and extremist groups to maintain power and control over a population. It is a threat to democracy, freedom, and human rights. It is essential that we as a society recognize the dangers of the nationalist narrative and work to combat it through education, open dialogue, and the protection of democratic institutions. We must also encourage critical thinking and reason, and not allow ourselves to be swayed by emotions and simplistic narratives. Only by doing so can we hope to build a more just and equitable society for all.

CASE STUDIES:

THE SLOW EROSION
How Democratic Institutions Are Being Hollowed Out

A Case Study of Recep Tayyip Erdoğan's Turkey

The health of a democracy is not measured solely by the presence of elections, but by the robustness of its institutions, the protection of minority rights, and the freedom of its citizens to express dissenting opinions without fear of reprisal. These pillars, which safeguard against tyranny and ensure accountability, are increasingly under threat globally, facing a subtle but persistent erosion that hollows out the very essence of democratic governance. This essay will explore this worrying trend, examining the mechanisms through which democratic institutions are being weakened, with a particular focus on the case of Recep Tayyip Erdoğan's Turkey. Once lauded as a model for democratic Islam, Turkey has witnessed a dramatic shift under Erdoğan's leadership, transitioning from a nation aspiring to join the European Union to a state characterized by authoritarian tendencies, suppressed dissent, and strained international relations.

The trajectory of Erdoğan's political career itself offers a crucial point of analysis. Initially, Erdoğan presented himself as a reformer, leading the

Justice and Development Party (AKP) to power in 2002 on a platform promising economic growth, EU accession, and democratic reforms. Early years saw significant progress, with the curtailment of the military's influence in politics, economic liberalization, and efforts to address the Kurdish issue. This earned him considerable support, both domestically and internationally. However, this reformer image began to unravel as Erdoğan consolidated his power and faced increasing challenges to his authority. This gradual transformation from a pro-democracy advocate to an increasingly authoritarian leader highlights a key vulnerability of democratic systems: the potential for charismatic leaders to exploit popular support and manipulate institutions to consolidate their personal power.

A watershed moment in Turkey's democratic backsliding was the attempted coup d'état in July 2016. While the coup itself was a direct attack on the democratically elected government, the response from Erdoğan and the AKP was far-reaching and arguably disproportionate, utilizing the event as a justification for a sweeping crackdown on dissent. The state of emergency that followed granted the government extraordinary powers, leading to the arbitrary arrest and detention of thousands of individuals, including journalists, academics, civil servants, and members of the judiciary. This purge, justified as necessary to root out alleged Gülenist sympathizers, effectively silenced critical voices and instilled a climate of fear within Turkish society. The sheer scale and arbitrary nature of these actions raised serious concerns about the rule of law and the protection of fundamental rights. This instance highlights a common tactic employed in the hollowing out of democratic institutions: leveraging a crisis, real or perceived, to justify the suspension of democratic norms and the suppression of opposition.

The control of the judiciary, a critical component of any functioning democracy, has been systematically undermined in Turkey. Following the coup attempt, thousands of judges and prosecutors were dismissed or arrested, often replaced by individuals perceived as loyal to the AKP. This politicization of the judiciary has eroded its independence and impartiality, making it increasingly difficult for citizens to seek redress against government actions and further entrenching executive power. The erosion of judicial independence is a particularly insidious form of democratic backsliding, as it undermines the very foundation of the rule of law and leaves citizens vulnerable to arbitrary state power. Without an independent judiciary to act as a check on executive overreach, the risk of abuse of power increases significantly.

The freedom of the media, essential for holding power accountable, has been severely curtailed. Numerous newspapers, television stations, and news agencies perceived as critical of the government have been shut down, often on dubious grounds of supporting terrorism. Journalists critical of Erdoğan and the AKP face intimidation, arrest, and prosecution. This suppression of independent media has created a highly controlled information environment, making it difficult for citizens to access diverse perspectives and holding the government accountable for its actions. The media's role as the "fourth estate" is crucial for a healthy democracy, and its silencing effectively muzzles public discourse and enables the government to operate with diminished transparency.

The strategic use of religious rhetoric has also played a significant role in consolidating Erdoğan's power. By appealing to conservative religious sentiments, the AKP has cultivated a strong base of support and framed dissent as an attack on traditional values and religious identity. This tactic has proved particularly effective in marginalizing secular and liberal voices within Turkish society and creating a sense of "us versus them," where opposition to the government is equated with opposition to the nation's core values. This manipulation of national and religious identity is a dangerous tool for silencing dissent and legitimizing authoritarian rule, fostering a climate of intolerance and division within society.

Finally, the shift in Turkish foreign policy further illustrates the hollowing out of democratic principles. Under Erdoğan, Turkey has increasingly distanced itself from its traditional Western allies, particularly the European Union and the United States, pursuing a more assertive and independent foreign policy. This shift has been accompanied by strained relations with European countries, particularly regarding human rights and democracy. While a degree of independent foreign policy is the prerogative of any sovereign nation, the growing authoritarianism within Turkey has made it increasingly difficult for Western democracies to engage constructively with the country, leading to further isolation and consolidation of autocratic tendencies.

In conclusion, the case of Recep Tayyip Erdoğan's Turkey provides a stark and alarming example of how democratic institutions can be systematically undermined and hollowed out from within. Through a combination of exploiting crises, manipulating legal frameworks, suppressing dissent, controlling the media, and leveraging religious rhetoric, Erdoğan has transformed Turkey from a promising democratic reformer to a state characterized by authoritarian tendencies and a weakened commitment to the rule of law. The Turkish experience serves as a cautionary tale, highlighting the fragility of democratic institutions and the ever-present need for vigilance in safeguarding them against manipulation and erosion. It underscores the importance of a robust civil society, an independent judiciary, a free press, and a politically engaged citizenry in preserving the health and vitality of democratic governance. The decline of democracy in Turkey is not simply a Turkish problem; it is a global concern that demands attention and a renewed commitment to defending democratic principles in the face of authoritarian challenges.

THE POPULIST PLAYBOOK
Exploiting Fear and Promising Salvation

Populism, a recurring phenomenon in political history, often presents itself as a champion of the "common person" against a perceived corrupt elite. While its initial appeal may stem from genuine grievances, a closer examination reveals a predictable playbook built on exploiting societal fears and promising simplistic, often unrealistic, solutions. This playbook, characterized by divisive rhetoric, the identification of scapegoats, and the promise of radical change, can have both short-term electoral success and long-term detrimental effects on democratic institutions.

One of the core tenets of the populist playbook is the **amplification of existing anxieties.** Populist leaders excel at identifying pre-existing societal fears – economic insecurity, cultural change, immigration, or perceived threats to national identity – and magnifying them for political gain. This is often achieved through emotionally charged language and the dissemination of narratives that paint a picture of impending doom if their proposed solutions are not implemented. For example, in times of economic hardship, a populist might focus on the threat of job losses due to globalization, portraying foreign nations or trade agreements as the primary cause, rather than addressing the complexities of technological change or domestic policy failures. The Brexit campaign in the UK, for instance, skillfully tapped into anxieties about immigration and national sovereignty, presenting leaving the European Union as the only way to "take back control."

Hand-in-hand with fear-mongering is the **creation of a clear "us vs. them" dichotomy.** Populist leaders thrive on dividing society into distinct groups: the "virtuous people" (often defined as the working class, the rural population, or a specific ethnic or national group) and the "corrupt elite" (politicians, intellectuals, the media, big business, or minority groups). This division simplifies complex issues and allows the populist to position themselves as the sole defender of the "true" people. This strategy often involves the use of derogatory terms and stereotypes to demonize the "other" group, fostering resentment and animosity. Think of the rhetoric employed against immigrants in various populist movements, often portraying them as a drain on resources or a threat to national culture, ignoring their potential contributions to society. This "us vs. them" mentality makes compromise and reasoned debate incredibly difficult, poisoning the political atmosphere.

Furthermore, the populist playbook relies heavily on the **identification of scapegoats.** When faced with complex problems, populists offer simple, often misleading, explanations, blaming specific individuals or groups for the woes of society. This deflects attention from systemic issues and allows the populist to avoid offering concrete solutions. Historically, scapegoats have included religious minorities, ethnic groups, and foreign powers. In the United States, Senator Joseph McCarthy's accusations of communist infiltration in the 1950s exemplify this tactic, as did the blaming of Jewish people for Germany's economic problems in the lead-up to World War II. The scapegoat becomes a convenient target for anger and frustration, creating a sense of unity among the "us" against a common enemy.

Beyond exploiting fear, populists also promise **radical salvation** – a quick and easy fix to deeply rooted problems. They often present themselves as strong leaders who can sweep away the old order and usher in a new era of prosperity and justice. This promise typically involves dramatic policy changes, often implemented without careful consideration of their long-term consequences. Promises to "drain the swamp," build walls, or drastically cut taxes appeal to a desire for quick fixes and decisive action, even if those solutions are impractical or unsustainable. This appeal to emotion often overshadows rational analysis and evidence-based policymaking.

The **psychological appeal** of populism is significant. In times of uncertainty and social upheaval, people crave a sense of order and control. Populist leaders offer a simplified worldview, providing clear answers and a sense of belonging. They often appeal to those who feel left behind or ignored by the mainstream political establishment. This sense of validation and empowerment can be incredibly attractive, particularly to those who feel marginalized or disenfranchised. Furthermore, the strong, charismatic leadership style often associated with populism can provide a sense of security and reassurance in an increasingly complex world.

The **consequences of following the populist playbook can be severe.** While populist movements can sometimes bring attention to legitimate grievances and force political systems to address neglected issues, they also pose a significant threat to democratic institutions. The erosion of trust in institutions, the suppression of dissent, the polarization of society, and the scapegoating of vulnerable groups can all undermine the foundations of a healthy democracy. Furthermore, the simplistic solutions offered by populists often fail to address the underlying problems, leading to disillusionment and further instability. Historically, populist movements have, in some cases, paved the way for authoritarian regimes.

So, how can societies **counter the appeal of the populist playbook?** The answer lies in promoting critical thinking, strengthening democratic institutions, addressing the root causes of social and economic inequality, and fostering a culture of empathy and understanding. A robust and independent media is crucial for holding populist leaders accountable and providing accurate information to the public. Education plays a vital role in equipping citizens with the skills to analyze information critically and resist manipulation. Furthermore, political leaders and civil society organizations must actively engage with those who feel marginalized and disenfranchised, addressing their concerns and offering constructive solutions. Ultimately, resisting the allure of the populist playbook requires a commitment to reasoned debate, evidence-based policymaking, and an unwavering defense of democratic values. Only through such efforts can we prevent the exploitation of fear and the false promise of salvation from undermining the foundations of a just and equitable society.

Let's explore the common tactics used by populist leaders: scapegoating, simplifying complex issues, and appealing to emotion over reason.

Populist leaders, who claim to represent the common person against the elite, often employ dangerous tactics to gain and maintain power. These tactics include scapegoating, simplifying complex issues, and appealing to emotions rather than reason. By understanding these strategies, we can better recognize and protect ourselves against the potential harm they may cause.

Scapegoating is a common tactic used by populist leaders to divert attention from their own failures or from more complex issues. By blaming a particular group for society's problems, these leaders create an "other" that is easily vilified and against whom their supporters can direct their anger and frustration. This tactic is not only divisive but also dangerous, as it can lead to discrimination, prejudice, and even violence against the targeted group. Moreover, scapegoating undermines the democratic process by shifting the focus from meaningful policy debates to misdirected blame.

Simplifying complex issues is another tactic employed by populist leaders to garner support. By providing oversimplified solutions to multifaceted problems, these leaders appeal to their supporters' desire for quick fixes. However, simplistic answers often fail to address the root causes of issues or consider the long-term consequences of their proposed solutions. This approach can lead to ineffective policies, as well as a lack of understanding and engagement from the public about the actual challenges their societies face.

Emotional appeals are at the heart of populist leaders' rhetoric. By tapping into their supporters' fears, anxieties, and prejudices, these leaders create a narrative that resonates with their base. Emotionally-charged language and imagery are used to elicit strong reactions and solidify group identity. However, this reliance on emotions over reason can lead to poor decision-making, as well as the marginalization of facts, expertise, and evidence-based policies.

To counter these dangerous tactics, it is crucial to promote critical thinking, education, and open dialogue. Encouraging citizens to scrutinize the messages of populist leaders, consider multiple perspectives, and seek out reliable information can help build resistance to manipulation. Furthermore, fostering an inclusive, tolerant, and diverse society can diminish the effectiveness of scapegoating and prejudice. By actively engaging in the democratic process, citizens can contribute to a more constructive and informed political environment.

In conclusion, populist leaders' tactics of scapegoating, oversimplification, and emotional appeals pose significant threats to democracy, social cohesion, and evidence-based policymaking. By recognizing these strategies and promoting critical thinking and open dialogue, we can work towards a more informed and engaged citizenry that resists manipulation and fosters a more inclusive and constructive political climate.

**Let's analyze the dangers of
"us vs. them" rhetoric
and the erosion of democratic norms.**

THE POISONED WELL
How "Us vs. Them" Rhetoric Undermines Democratic Norms

The health and vitality of any democracy depend on a shared commitment to civil discourse, reasoned debate, and a willingness to find common ground. However, these foundations are increasingly threatened by the pervasive adoption of "us vs. them" rhetoric, a divisive strategy that casts society as a battleground between opposing groups, fostering animosity, and ultimately eroding the very democratic norms that underpin a free society. This essay will analyze the insidious dangers inherent in this type of rhetoric, exploring how it manipulates emotions, distorts reality, and paves the way for authoritarian tendencies.

The core danger of "us vs. them" thinking lies in its simplification of complex issues. Nuance is sacrificed at the altar of emotional appeal, and individuals are reduced to caricatures defined solely by their perceived affiliation with the "other." This binary framework, often fueled by fear and resentment, prevents meaningful dialogue and critical thinking. When issues are framed as zero-sum games, where one group's gain is inherently another's loss, compromise becomes impossible and cooperation falls by the wayside. Instead, the focus shifts to demonizing the opposition and consolidating power within the "us" group.

This type of rhetoric typically relies on several manipulative techniques. First, it often employs scapegoating, identifying a specific group as the source of all societal ills. This tactic redirects anger and frustration away from systemic problems and towards a readily identifiable target, thus deflecting responsibility and hindering genuine solutions. Historically, marginalized communities have frequently been targeted as scapegoats, bearing the brunt of economic hardship, social anxieties, and political instability.

Second, "us vs. them" rhetoric leverages identity politics to create artificial divisions. It emphasizes differences in race, religion, ethnicity, or ideology to construct solid boundaries between groups, even when shared interests and values may exist. This emphasis on difference obscures shared humanity and fosters distrust, making it more difficult to build bridges and foster empathy. Social media platforms, with their echo chambers and algorithmic amplification of extreme views, have become fertile ground for this type of divisive rhetoric.

Third, it frequently involves the deliberate spread of misinformation and disinformation. Creating a narrative that paints the "them" group as deceitful, malicious, and dangerous justifies extreme measures to defend the "us." This often leads to the erosion of trust in institutions like the media, the scientific community, and the electoral system itself. When objective truth becomes contested and alternative realities proliferate, the common ground necessary for democratic governance disappears.

The historical record is replete with examples of how "us vs. them" rhetoric has fueled conflict, oppression, and even genocide. From the anti-Semitic propaganda of Nazi Germany to the dehumanization of ethnic minorities in the Rwandan genocide, the consequences of fostering such divisions are devastatingly clear. In these cases, the language of hatred and exclusion paved the way for unspeakable atrocities.

Furthermore, the normalization of "us vs. them" thinking erodes specific democratic norms crucial for a healthy political system. The principle of tolerance, which requires respecting the rights and beliefs of those with whom we disagree, becomes increasingly difficult to uphold. Free and fair elections, a cornerstone of democracy, are undermined when the legitimacy of the opposition is questioned and attempts are made to disenfranchise or marginalize certain groups. The rule of law, which ensures that everyone is subject to the same legal standards, is compromised when the "us" group is seen as above the law or when the "them" group is denied equal protection under the law.

The increasing polarization of the media landscape further exacerbates the problem. News outlets and online platforms often cater to specific ideological groups, reinforcing pre-existing biases and limiting exposure to diverse perspectives. This creates echo chambers where individuals are primarily exposed to information that confirms their existing beliefs, further solidifying their "us vs. them" worldview.

Combating the dangers of "us vs. them" rhetoric requires a multi-faceted approach. First, it is essential to promote media literacy and critical thinking skills, enabling individuals to discern credible sources of information from misinformation and propaganda. Second, fostering genuine dialogue and cross-cultural understanding is crucial for breaking down stereotypes and building empathy across different groups. Third, political leaders and influencers must be held accountable for using divisive language and promoting harmful stereotypes. Finally, strengthening democratic institutions and ensuring equal access to justice and opportunity for all members of society can help to address the underlying grievances that fuel resentment and division.

In conclusion, "us vs. them" rhetoric poses a significant threat to the foundations of democratic societies. By simplifying complex issues, manipulating emotions, and eroding trust in institutions, it undermines the very principles of tolerance, inclusivity, and reasoned debate that are essential for a healthy and vibrant democracy. Recognizing the dangers of this rhetoric and actively promoting empathy, understanding, and critical thinking are crucial steps in safeguarding the future of democratic governance. Only by rejecting the poisonous well of division can we hope to build a society where all individuals are treated with dignity and respect, and where common ground can be found in the pursuit of a more just and equitable future for all.

CASE STUDIES:

BRAZIL
THE BOLSONARO ERA
A Deep Dive into Populism's Rise and Repercussions

The rise and tenure of Jair Bolsonaro as President of Brazil (2019-2022) represents a pivotal moment in the nation's modern history, a period characterized by a sharp turn towards right-wing populism and a significant reshaping of its political, economic, and social landscape. Understanding the Bolsonaro era requires analyzing the historical context that facilitated his ascent, dissecting his leadership profile and populist strategies, and critically examining the concrete policies he implemented and their wide-ranging consequences. This case study will delve into each of these facets, providing concrete examples and evidence to paint a comprehensive picture of this transformative — and often controversial — period in Brazilian history.

HISTORICAL CONTEXT:
A Fertile Ground for Populism

Bolsonaro's rise to power was not a sudden anomaly but rather the culmination of a series of crises and disillusionments that had deeply eroded public trust in Brazil's established institutions. Two key factors stand out: widespread corruption scandals and a prolonged economic recession, both intertwined with a growing sense of social polarization.

The "Lava Jato" (Car Wash) operation, a massive anti-corruption investigation launched in 2014, uncovered a web of bribery and kickbacks involving prominent politicians, business leaders, and state-owned companies like Petrobras. This scandal, while initially lauded for its pursuit of justice, ultimately implicated figures across the political spectrum, fueling widespread public cynicism and a deep-seated distrust of the traditional political class. The Workers' Party (PT), which had governed Brazil for over a decade, was particularly hard hit, with its leading figures, including former President Lula da Silva, facing legal challenges. This created a vacuum of leadership and a yearning for an outsider figure who could cleanse the system of its perceived corruption.

Concurrently, Brazil faced a severe economic recession, triggered in 2014 and exacerbated by political instability. The economic downturn led to soaring unemployment, rising inflation, and a general sense of economic insecurity. This hardship further fueled public discontent and created a fertile ground for populist rhetoric that promised quick fixes and a return to prosperity. These economic anxieties, coupled with the outrage over corruption, amplified existing social divisions. The left-leaning policies of the PT era, while lauded for reducing poverty, were increasingly criticized by conservative sectors as being unsustainable and promoting excessive government intervention. This resulted in a polarized political climate where dialogue and compromise became increasingly difficult, paving the way for a leader who could capitalize on these divisions.

LEADERSHIP PROFILE:
The Making of a Right-Wing Populist

Jair Bolsonaro possessed a unique profile that resonated with specific segments of the Brazilian population. A former army captain with a 27-year career in Congress, he cultivated an image as a political outsider who was not afraid to challenge the status quo. His ideology can be broadly characterized as right-wing, nationalist, and conservative, encompassing elements of social conservatism, economic liberalism, and a strong emphasis on national security.

Bolsonaro's core ideology revolves around a nostalgic vision of Brazil's military dictatorship (1964-1985), often glorifying its authoritarian rule as a period of order and progress. He espoused traditional family values, fiercely opposed abortion and LGBTQ+ rights, and advocated for a tough-on-crime approach to address rising crime rates. His nationalist rhetoric emphasized Brazilian sovereignty and criticized globalization, often framing international agreements as threats to national interests. Economically, Bolsonaro embraced a neo-liberal agenda, advocating for deregulation, privatization, and austerity measures to reduce government debt and stimulate economic growth.

Key campaign promises included combating corruption, restoring law and order, and revitalizing the Brazilian economy. He pledged to crack down on crime by loosening gun control laws, empowering law enforcement, and increasing penalties for criminals. He promised to simplify the tax system, reduce government bureaucracy, and attract foreign investment through privatization and deregulation. Crucially, he presented himself as the antithesis of the PT and the perceived leftist establishment, appealing to voters who felt alienated by the prevailing political narrative.

POPULIST STRATEGIES:
Mastering the Art of Divisive Appeal

Bolsonaro's success was undeniably linked to his mastery of populist communication strategies, particularly his skillful use of social media, his relentless attacks on the media and political opponents, and his calculated appeal to nationalist sentiments.

He understood the power of social media in bypassing traditional media gatekeepers and directly engaging with his supporters. He cultivated a highly active online presence, utilizing platforms like Facebook, Twitter, and WhatsApp to disseminate his message, mobilize his base, and shape public opinion. His communication style was often unfiltered, incendiary, and deliberately provocative, designed to generate attention and rally his followers. He skillfully used social media to spread misinformation and conspiracy theories, undermining the credibility of his opponents and creating an echo chamber of support.

Simultaneously, Bolsonaro consistently attacked the mainstream media, accusing them of bias and fabricating news to undermine his presidency. He labeled critical journalists as "enemies of the people" and encouraged his supporters to distrust their reporting. This erosion of trust in the media further solidified his control over the narrative and allowed him to present an alternative version of reality to his followers.

Furthermore, Bolsonaro expertly appealed to nationalist sentiments by invoking symbols of Brazilian identity, such as the flag, the national anthem, and a romanticized vision of the country's past. He tapped into a sense of national pride and resentment towards perceived foreign interference, framing his policies as necessary to defend Brazil's sovereignty and interests. He also capitalized on anxieties about cultural changes and the perceived threat to traditional values, resonating with socially conservative voters who felt their way of life was under attack.

POLICIES AND CONSEQUENCES:
A Tangible Impact on Brazil

Bolsonaro's policies, rooted in his right-wing ideology, had a profound and often detrimental impact on Brazil across economic, social, and political spheres.

Economic: His administration pursued a policy of aggressive deregulation and privatization, particularly in the environmental sector. While proponents argued that these measures would attract investment and stimulate economic growth, they also led to a significant weakening of environmental regulations and a surge in deforestation, particularly in the Amazon rainforest. Statistics from Brazil's National Institute for Space Research (INPE) revealed a dramatic increase in deforestation rates during Bolsonaro's tenure, reaching record levels and drawing international condemnation. Austerity measures, while aimed at reducing government debt, disproportionately affected vulnerable populations by cutting social programs and limiting access to healthcare and education. While some economic indicators showed modest improvements, inequality remained persistent, and the benefits of economic growth were not evenly distributed.

Social: Bolsonaro's presidency was marked by a significant deterioration in social inclusion and human rights. His administration actively restricted the activities of civil society organizations, particularly those working on environmental protection and indigenous rights. He routinely attacked minority groups, including LGBTQ+ individuals and indigenous populations, using inflammatory rhetoric and discriminatory policies. Funding for programs supporting indigenous communities was drastically cut, and land rights claims were undermined, leading to increased violence and land grabbing in indigenous territories. His policies exacerbated existing social divisions and created a climate of fear and intolerance.

Political: Bolsonaro's tenure witnessed a gradual erosion of democratic norms and institutions. He openly questioned the integrity of the electoral system, echoing unsubstantiated claims of voter fraud and raising concerns about a potential challenge to the results of the 2022 election. He frequently attacked the judiciary, accusing judges of political bias and undermining their authority. He also weakened environmental regulations, making it easier for businesses to exploit natural resources and contributing to the devastation of the Amazon rainforest. His administration's actions raised serious concerns about the future of democracy in Brazil and its commitment to the rule of law.

Evidence and Examples: Illustrating the Key Trends

Numerous examples and pieces of evidence corroborate the claims made thus far:

Deforestation Statistics: INPE data consistently showed a sharp increase in deforestation rates in the Amazon rainforest during Bolsonaro's presidency, reaching record highs in 2019, 2020, and 2021.

Bolsonaro's Quotes: Public statements by Bolsonaro, such as his remark that "the environment is not a priority," clearly indicated his administration's disregard for environmental protection. His repeated attacks on the media and his questioning of the electoral system further exemplified his disdain for democratic norms.

Policy Analysis: The dismantling of environmental protection agencies and the weakening of environmental regulations, as documented by independent researchers and environmental organizations, directly contributed to the increase in deforestation and other environmental damage. The reduction in funding for social programs and indigenous communities had a demonstrable impact on their well-being and access to essential services.

International Condemnation: International organizations, such as the United Nations and human rights groups, issued numerous reports condemning Bolsonaro's policies on human rights, environmental protection, and indigenous rights. These reports provided further evidence of the negative consequences of his administration's actions.

A LEGACY OF DIVISION
and Uncertainty

The Bolsonaro era in Brazil was a period of profound transformation, characterized by a shift towards right-wing populism and a significant reshaping of the country's political, economic, and social landscape. While Bolsonaro's presidency resonated with specific segments of the Brazilian population, particularly those who felt alienated by the traditional political class, his policies had a detrimental impact on environmental protection, human rights, and democratic institutions. His populist strategies, including his skillful use of social media, his attacks on the media, and his appeal to nationalist sentiments, exacerbated existing social divisions and created a climate of polarization and distrust.

The long-term consequences of the Bolsonaro era remain to be seen. While the election of Luiz Inácio Lula da Silva in 2022 offered a potential course correction, the deep-seated divisions and institutional damage left behind by Bolsonaro will pose significant challenges for the new administration. Rebuilding trust in democratic institutions, addressing the environmental crisis, and promoting social inclusion will require a concerted effort to heal the wounds of the past and forge a more inclusive and sustainable future for Brazil. The Bolsonaro era serves as a stark reminder of the perils of populism and the importance of safeguarding democratic values, protecting human rights, and preserving the environment. It is a chapter in Brazilian history that demands careful analysis and critical reflection to prevent the recurrence of such a divisive and damaging period.

THE DIGITAL DICTATORSHIP
Surveillance and Control in the 21st Century

Let's explore how technology is being used to monitor, censor, and control populations.

The 21st century, heralded as an era of unprecedented connectivity and freedom of information, has ironically also witnessed the rise of a new form of authoritarianism: the digital dictatorship. Fueled by advancements in technology, governments and corporations are increasingly employing sophisticated surveillance techniques to monitor, censor, and ultimately control populations. This essay will explore the multifaceted ways in which technology is being weaponized against individual liberties, outlining the mechanisms of this digital control and analyzing its potential long-term consequences for democracy and human rights.

One of the most prominent features of the digital dictatorship is pervasive surveillance. The ubiquity of smartphones, social media platforms, and internet-connected devices has created a vast network of data points that can be collected, analyzed, and used to track individuals' movements, communications, and online activities. Facial recognition technology, coupled with extensive CCTV networks, allows for the real-time identification and tracking of people in public spaces. Algorithms can analyze online behavior to predict future actions, identify potential dissidents, and target individuals with personalized propaganda.

This constant monitoring stifles freedom of expression and assembly. Knowing that their online activities are being scrutinized, individuals may self-censor their opinions and avoid participating in activities deemed subversive by the authorities. The chilling effect of surveillance can discourage dissent and create a climate of fear, effectively silencing critical voices and suppressing political opposition. The potential for misuse of this data is immense, ranging from discriminatory practices based on profiling to the targeting of activists and journalists who challenge the status quo.

Beyond surveillance, digital dictatorships leverage technology to censor information and control the narrative. Governments can block access to websites, filter search results, and manipulate social media algorithms to promote their own agenda and suppress dissenting viewpoints. Social media platforms, while ostensibly designed for open communication, can be used to spread propaganda, disinformation, and hate speech. Bots and trolls can be deployed to harass individuals, silence opposing voices, and manipulate public opinion.

The sophistication of censorship techniques is constantly evolving. Deepfake technology, for example, allows for the creation of realistic but entirely fabricated videos and audio recordings, which can be used to discredit political opponents or spread false narratives. The ability to seamlessly manipulate information undermines trust in legitimate sources and makes it increasingly difficult for citizens to discern truth from falsehood. This erosion of trust in institutions and information further weakens democratic processes and empowers authoritarian regimes.

Perhaps the most concerning aspect of the digital dictatorship is its potential to create a system of social control that extends beyond the physical realm. Social credit systems, already implemented in some countries, monitor and evaluate citizens' behavior based on a variety of factors, including online activities, financial transactions, and social interactions. Individuals with low social credit scores may face restrictions on their access to education, employment, travel, and other essential services. This system effectively incentivizes conformity and discourages any behavior that could be deemed critical or disobedient.

The implications of this digital control are profound. It threatens the very foundations of democracy, which relies on freedom of expression, assembly, and access to information. When citizens are constantly monitored, censored, and manipulated, they are unable to make informed decisions and participate meaningfully in the political process. The potential for abuse of power is immense, and the lack of transparency and accountability in these systems makes it difficult to challenge the actions of authoritarian regimes.

However, the rise of the digital dictatorship is not inevitable. There are steps that can be taken to resist this trend and protect individual liberties in the digital age. Firstly, it is crucial to raise awareness about the dangers of surveillance and censorship. Education and public discourse are essential to inform citizens about the techniques being used to control them and the potential consequences for their freedom.

Secondly, we need to advocate for strong legal protections for privacy and freedom of expression. Laws must be enacted to limit the collection and use of personal data, regulate the use of facial recognition technology, and protect individuals from online censorship and harassment. These laws must be enforced effectively and provide avenues for redress for those whose rights have been violated.

Thirdly, we need to support the development of technologies that promote privacy and security. Encrypted communication tools, decentralized social media platforms, and privacy-enhancing technologies can help individuals protect their online activities from surveillance and censorship. These tools must be accessible and user-friendly to empower citizens to take control of their digital lives.

Finally, international cooperation is essential to combat the rise of the digital dictatorship. Governments, civil society organizations, and technology companies must work together to promote human rights and democratic values in the digital realm. International norms and standards must be established to regulate the use of technology and prevent its abuse by authoritarian regimes.

In conclusion, the digital dictatorship represents a serious threat to individual liberties and democratic values in the 21st century. By leveraging technology for surveillance, censorship, and social control, authoritarian regimes are attempting to silence dissent, manipulate public opinion, and maintain their grip on power. However, by raising awareness, advocating for legal protections, supporting the development of privacy-enhancing technologies, and fostering international cooperation, we can resist this trend and ensure that technology is used to empower individuals rather than control them. The future of democracy depends on our ability to defend our digital rights and freedoms in the face of this growing threat. The fight for a free and open internet is a fight for the very soul of the 21st century.

THE ALL-SEEING EYE
Analyzing the Rise
of Surveillance States *and the*
Erosion of Privacy Rights

The 21st century is increasingly defined by a tension between security and liberty, a conflict starkly manifested in the rise of surveillance states across the globe. While governments argue that enhanced monitoring is crucial to combating terrorism, crime, and social unrest, the expansion of surveillance capabilities has led to a significant erosion of privacy rights, raising profound questions about the future of democratic societies and individual autonomy. This essay will analyze the multifaceted forces driving the proliferation of surveillance technologies, examine the impact on fundamental rights, and consider the potential consequences for freedom of expression, political dissent, and the very fabric of social life.

One of the primary drivers of the surveillance state is the pervasive availability of advanced technology. The digital revolution has provided governments with unprecedented tools for collecting, storing, and analyzing vast amounts of data. From CCTV cameras blanketing urban landscapes to sophisticated algorithms capable of tracking online activity, the technical capacity for mass surveillance has far outstripped legal and ethical frameworks designed to protect individual privacy. The rise of social media platforms, while fostering connection and communication, has also created a readily accessible trove of personal information that can be mined by state actors for various purposes, often without the explicit consent or knowledge of the individuals involved. Furthermore, advancements in biometric technologies, such as facial recognition, allow for the real-time identification and tracking of individuals in public spaces, blurring the lines between public safety and constant monitoring.

The justification for increased surveillance often centers on the perceived need to enhance national security. In the wake of terrorist attacks and heightened geopolitical instability, governments have argued that intrusive surveillance measures are necessary to prevent future threats. The "war on terror," in particular, has been instrumental in legitimizing the expansion of surveillance powers, often through the passage of legislation that grants broad authority to intelligence agencies. However, critics argue that such measures can be easily abused and disproportionately target marginalized communities, leading to discriminatory practices and the erosion of civil liberties for all citizens. The potential for mission creep, where surveillance technologies initially intended for counter-terrorism are repurposed for other purposes, such as policing minor offenses or suppressing political dissent, is a significant concern.

The impact of surveillance on privacy rights is profound and far-reaching. The constant monitoring of citizens can create a chilling effect on freedom of expression, as individuals may be less likely to voice dissenting opinions or engage in political activism if they fear being watched or targeted. The knowledge that one's online activity is being tracked can also lead to self-censorship and a reluctance to explore diverse viewpoints, ultimately stifling intellectual curiosity and hindering the free exchange of ideas. Furthermore, the collection and storage of personal data raise concerns about data security and the potential for misuse or abuse. Data breaches, hacking incidents, and the unauthorized sharing of information can expose individuals to identity theft, financial fraud, and other forms of harm.

The rise of surveillance states also raises important questions about the role of corporations in facilitating and perpetuating these practices. Many tech companies collect and store vast amounts of user data, which can be accessed by governments through legal or extralegal means. The close relationship between Silicon Valley and intelligence agencies has fueled concerns about the potential for collusion and the blurring of lines between the public and private sectors. The debate over encryption, for example, highlights the tension between law enforcement's desire to access encrypted communications and the right of individuals to protect their privacy through secure communication channels.

Addressing the challenges posed by the surveillance state requires a multi-pronged approach. Strong legal frameworks are needed to regulate the collection, storage, and use of personal data, ensuring transparency and accountability. Independent oversight bodies should be established to monitor the activities of intelligence agencies and prevent abuses of power. Furthermore, individuals need to be empowered to protect their privacy through education and access to tools that enhance anonymity and security. Promoting digital literacy and critical thinking skills is essential to fostering a citizenry that is aware of the risks of surveillance and capable of making informed choices about their online behavior.

The rise of surveillance states represents a significant threat to privacy rights and democratic values. While security concerns are legitimate, they should not come at the expense of fundamental freedoms. A balance must be struck between protecting national security and safeguarding individual liberties. This requires a commitment to transparency, accountability, and the rule of law, as well as a robust public debate about the ethical and societal implications of surveillance technologies. The future of freedom depends on our ability to navigate this complex landscape and ensure that technology serves to empower, rather than control, the individual. Only then can we hope to build a society where security and liberty coexist.

THE LABYRINTH OF LIES
Navigating the Challenges of Fighting Disinformation *in the* Digital Age

The digital age, heralded as a period of unprecedented access to information and global connectivity, has ironically ushered in a parallel era: the age of disinformation. A complex web of fabricated narratives, deliberately misleading content, and manipulated facts now permeates our online spaces, posing a significant threat to informed decision-making, democratic processes, and even social cohesion. Fighting this insidious phenomenon presents a formidable challenge, requiring a multi-faceted approach that addresses the technological advancements enabling its spread, the psychological vulnerabilities that make us susceptible to it, and the societal consequences it engenders.

One of the primary challenges lies in the sheer **scale and velocity** of disinformation proliferation. Social media platforms, with their algorithms designed to maximize engagement, often amplify sensational or emotionally charged content, regardless of its veracity. This creates an echo chamber effect, where individuals are primarily exposed to information confirming their pre-existing beliefs, reinforcing biases and making them less receptive to alternative perspectives and factual corrections. The ease with which sophisticated bots and fake accounts can be created and deployed further exacerbates the problem, allowing malicious actors to rapidly disseminate disinformation campaigns designed to manipulate public opinion or sow discord. Imagine a coordinated effort, thousands of accounts simultaneously pushing a narrative, effectively drowning out legitimate sources of information and shaping the online discourse. This is a reality we grapple with daily, a constant barrage of manipulated narratives vying for attention.

The **evolving sophistication of disinformation techniques** poses a constant challenge to detection and mitigation efforts. Simple, easily debunked falsehoods are increasingly being replaced by more insidious methods like deepfakes, which utilize artificial intelligence to create realistic but entirely fabricated videos and audio recordings. These deceptive technologies blur the lines between reality and fiction, making it incredibly difficult for even discerning individuals to distinguish between genuine and manipulated content. The use of context manipulation, where genuine information is strategically altered or presented out of context to promote a specific agenda, is another prevalent tactic. This subtlety makes it harder to identify the falsehood, as fragments of truth are woven into a fabric of deception. The constant innovation in these techniques necessitates a continuous arms race, requiring constant updates to detection algorithms and fact-checking methodologies.

Another significant challenge is the **psychological vulnerability** of individuals to disinformation. Cognitive biases, such as confirmation bias (seeking out information that confirms existing beliefs) and negativity bias (being more attentive to negative information), make us more susceptible to accepting and sharing false or misleading content. Confirmation bias often leads individuals to selectively consume information that reinforces their viewpoints, regardless of its accuracy. This creates filter bubbles, where individuals are shielded from opposing arguments and become more entrenched in their beliefs. Negativity bias, on the other hand, makes us more likely to remember and share negative stories, even if they are false. The emotional resonance of disinformation, particularly when it taps into fears, anxieties, or prejudices, also makes it more likely to go viral, bypassing rational analysis and critical thinking. Understanding these psychological mechanisms is crucial in developing effective strategies to combat the spread of disinformation, focusing on promoting media literacy and critical thinking skills.

Beyond the technological and psychological challenges, the **lack of consensus on what constitutes disinformation and who should be responsible for combating it** further complicates the issue. Defining disinformation can be a contentious process, as it often overlaps with legitimate forms of expression, opinion, and satire. Overly broad definitions can lead to censorship and the suppression of legitimate viewpoints, while overly narrow definitions may fail to capture the full scope of the problem. The question of responsibility is equally complex. Should social media platforms be solely responsible for policing their content, or should governments play a more active role? Balancing the need to combat disinformation with the protection of freedom of speech is a delicate act, requiring careful consideration of the potential consequences of each approach. A collaborative effort involving stakeholders from various sectors, including tech companies, government agencies, educational institutions, and civil society organizations, is essential to develop effective and ethical strategies for addressing this challenge.

Finally, the **global nature of disinformation campaigns** presents a significant hurdle. Disinformation can originate from anywhere in the world, targeting individuals and communities across national borders. This makes it difficult to track the source of disinformation and hold those responsible accountable. Moreover, different countries have different laws and regulations regarding freedom of speech and online content, further complicating efforts to combat disinformation internationally. International cooperation is essential to address this challenge, requiring the development of common standards and protocols for identifying and combating disinformation across borders.

This includes sharing information about disinformation campaigns, coordinating enforcement actions, and promoting media literacy education globally.

Fighting disinformation in the digital age is a multifaceted and complex challenge that requires a comprehensive and collaborative approach. Addressing the technological advancements that enable its spread, understanding the psychological vulnerabilities that make us susceptible to it, and developing ethical and effective strategies for combating it are all essential steps in protecting ourselves and our societies from the insidious effects of disinformation. The stakes are high, as the erosion of trust in institutions, the polarization of societies, and the undermining of democratic processes all threaten the foundations of a healthy and informed society. By fostering media literacy, promoting critical thinking skills, and working together to create a more resilient information ecosystem, we can navigate the labyrinth of lies and build a future where truth prevails.

CASE STUDIES:

CHINA'S SOCIAL CREDIT SYSTEM: A Double-Edged Sword of Information Control

China's social credit system, still under development, aims to create a comprehensive score for each citizen based on their behavior, both online and offline. This score can then be used to grant or deny access to various services, such as loans, travel, and education. While proponents argue that the system promotes social harmony and trustworthiness, critics raise concerns about its potential for abuse and its chilling effect on freedom of expression.

The social credit system relies heavily on data collection and surveillance, raising serious privacy concerns. Information gathered from various sources, including online activity, financial transactions, and even social interactions, is used to assess an individual's "creditworthiness." This creates a powerful incentive for citizens to conform to government-approved behavior, even if it means self-censorship or suppressing dissenting opinions.

Moreover, the system is vulnerable to errors and biases. Algorithms used to calculate social credit scores may inadvertently penalize individuals based on inaccurate or incomplete information. This can lead to unfair consequences and erode public trust in the system. The lack of transparency and due process in the system further exacerbates these concerns.

While the social credit system is not explicitly designed to spread disinformation, its inherent control over information and behavior can indirectly contribute to the problem. By incentivizing conformity and discouraging dissent, the system can create an environment where critical thinking is suppressed and alternative viewpoints are marginalized. This can make it easier for the government to control the narrative and disseminate its own version of events, potentially leading to a distorted understanding of reality.

RUSSIA'S ONLINE MANIPULATION TACTICS: Weaponizing Information for Geopolitical Gain

Russia has been widely accused of using online manipulation tactics to interfere in elections, sow discord, and undermine democratic institutions in other countries. These tactics include the creation and dissemination of fake news, the use of social media bots and trolls to amplify divisive messages, and the hacking and leaking of sensitive information.

The Russian government has been accused of supporting "troll farms" that employ individuals to create and spread disinformation on social media platforms. These trolls often pose as ordinary citizens and engage in online conversations to promote pro-Russian narratives, spread conspiracy theories, and sow discord among opposing political groups. They use sophisticated techniques to evade detection, such as using proxy servers to mask their location and creating fake social media profiles with stolen or fabricated identities.

Furthermore, Russian hackers have been accused of targeting government agencies, political organizations, and media outlets to steal sensitive information and leak it online. This information is often selectively edited or manipulated to create a false narrative and damage the reputation of targeted individuals or organizations.

The impact of Russia's online manipulation tactics has been significant. These tactics have been shown to influence public opinion, exacerbate political divisions, and undermine trust in democratic institutions. The spread of disinformation has also been linked to real-world violence and unrest.

Both China's social credit system and Russia's online manipulation tactics highlight the complex challenges of fighting disinformation in the digital age. These case studies demonstrate how technology can be used to control information, manipulate public opinion, and undermine democratic institutions.

Addressing these challenges requires a multi-faceted approach that includes:

- **Strengthening media literacy and critical thinking skills**: Educating individuals on how to evaluate online sources, identify biases, and distinguish between credible and unreliable information is crucial.

- **Promoting transparency and accountability on social media platforms**: Social media companies need to be more transparent about their algorithms and content moderation policies, and they need to be held accountable for the spread of disinformation on their platforms.

- **Supporting independent journalism and fact-checking organizations**: Independent journalism and fact-checking organizations play a vital role in holding power accountable and debunking false information.

- **Developing international norms and standards for online behavior:** International cooperation is needed to develop norms and standards for online behavior that respect freedom of expression while also protecting against the spread of disinformation.

- **Investing in research and development of new technologies to detect and counter disinformation**: New technologies, such as artificial intelligence, can be used to detect and counter disinformation more effectively.

The fight against disinformation is an ongoing challenge that requires a concerted effort from governments, social media platforms, media organizations, and individuals. By working together, we can create a more informed and resilient society that is better equipped to navigate the complexities of the digital age. Only through constant vigilance, proactive measures, and a commitment to truth can we hope to tame the hydra of disinformation and preserve the integrity of our information ecosystem.

THE EROSION OF INSTITUTIONS
Undermining the Pillars of Democracy

Democracy, in its purest form, relies not merely on the will of the people, but also on a complex network of institutions designed to translate that will into effective and equitable governance. These institutions – the judiciary, the legislature, the executive, the free press, and civil society organizations – act as vital pillars, supporting the structure of a democratic society and ensuring its stability. However, in recent years, we have witnessed an alarming trend: the erosion of these institutions, a phenomenon that threatens the very foundations of democracy itself. This erosion manifests in various forms, from blatant attacks on the independence of the judiciary to subtle but corrosive manipulations of the electoral process, ultimately undermining public trust and paving the way for authoritarianism.

The health of a democracy is directly proportional to the strength and integrity of its institutions. They provide checks and balances, preventing any single branch of government from accumulating excessive power. They ensure accountability, holding leaders responsible for their actions and protecting citizens from abuse. They foster transparency, allowing the public to access information and participate in the decision-making process. When these institutions are weakened, the safeguards against tyranny crumble, leaving the door open for corruption, abuse of power, and the suppression of dissent.

One of the most concerning aspects of institutional erosion is the undermining of the **judiciary**. An independent judiciary is the cornerstone of the rule of law, ensuring equal application of justice and protecting individual rights. However, we see increasing instances of political interference in judicial appointments, attempts to discredit judges who rule against the government, and deliberate underfunding of the court system. These actions erode public confidence in the judiciary's impartiality, leading to a perception that justice is not blind but rather swayed by political considerations. This can have a chilling effect on those seeking redress for grievances and embolden those who believe they can operate with impunity.

Furthermore, the **legislative branch**, the body responsible for representing the people's will and enacting laws, is often subjected to manipulation and obstruction. Gerrymandering, the practice of drawing electoral district boundaries to favor one party, distorts the representation of voters and creates safe seats for incumbents, reducing accountability. The proliferation of partisan gridlock, fueled by increasing political polarization, prevents meaningful legislation from being passed, rendering the legislative branch ineffective. Moreover, the spread of disinformation and the influence of dark money in elections further undermine the integrity of the legislative process, allowing special interests to dictate policy decisions.

The **executive branch**, arguably the most powerful arm of government, is not immune to the erosion of institutional norms. The concentration of power in the executive, often justified by appeals to efficiency or national security, can lead to abuses and overreach. The appointment of loyalists rather than qualified experts to key positions, the politicization of government agencies, and the erosion of civil service protections all contribute to a weakening of institutional expertise and a decline in the quality of governance. Furthermore, the use of executive orders and other unilateral actions bypasses the legislative process and undermines the principle of separation of powers.

A free and independent **press** is essential for holding power accountable and informing the public. However, the media landscape is increasingly under pressure from government interference, economic challenges, and the spread of misinformation. Governments may attempt to control the flow of information through censorship, intimidation, or the manipulation of state-owned media. Economic pressures, such as the decline of traditional media revenue models, can lead to consolidation and a narrowing of perspectives. The proliferation of fake news and propaganda on social media platforms further erodes public trust in credible news sources and makes it increasingly difficult for citizens to distinguish between fact and fiction. This ultimately undermines the ability of the public to make informed decisions and hold their leaders accountable.

Finally, the health of **civil society organizations** is crucial for a vibrant democracy. These organizations play a vital role in advocating for citizen interests, holding government accountable, and providing essential services. However, they are often targeted by governments seeking to suppress dissent or silence critical voices. Restrictive laws, such as those limiting funding or freedom of assembly, can cripple civil society organizations and prevent them from effectively performing their functions. The demonization of civil society groups as "enemies of the state" further undermines their legitimacy and discourages public support.

The consequences of institutional erosion are far-reaching. It leads to a decline in public trust in government, a rise in political polarization, and an increase in corruption and abuse of power. When people lose faith in the institutions designed to protect them, they become disillusioned and disengaged, creating a vacuum that can be filled by authoritarian forces. The erosion of institutions can also lead to economic instability, social unrest, and even violent conflict.

Reversing this trend requires a concerted effort from all stakeholders. Governments must commit to strengthening institutional independence, promoting transparency, and upholding the rule of law. Civil society organizations must continue to advocate for institutional reform and hold those in power accountable. The media must remain vigilant in exposing corruption and providing accurate and unbiased information. And citizens must become more engaged in the political process, demanding accountability from their leaders and supporting policies that promote institutional integrity.

Ultimately, the survival of democracy depends on the strength and resilience of its institutions. By recognizing the signs of institutional erosion and taking action to address them, we can safeguard the pillars of democracy and ensure a more just and equitable future for all. The fight to preserve and strengthen these institutions is not just a political battle; it is a moral imperative. It is a fight for the very soul of democracy and the future of self-governance. Only through vigilance, commitment, and collective action can we prevent the erosion of our institutions from undermining the foundations of our democratic society.

THE EROSION OF INDEPENDENCE
How Authoritarian Regimes Subvert Key Institutions

Authoritarian regimes, by their very nature, stand in stark opposition to the principles of transparency, accountability, and pluralism that underpin a healthy democracy. A key strategy employed by such regimes to maintain and consolidate power involves the systematic weakening of independent institutions. These institutions – the judiciary, the press, and civil society organizations (CSOs) – serve as vital checks on governmental power, providing avenues for dissent, oversight, and the protection of individual rights. Authoritarian leaders recognize these institutions as threats and, therefore, actively seek to neutralize their influence through a variety of methods.

One of the primary targets is the **judiciary**. An independent judiciary, capable of impartially interpreting laws and holding the government accountable, directly challenges the arbitrary exercise of power central to authoritarian rule. Regimes often undermine judicial independence through several tactics. Political appointments are a common tool, where judges are selected based on their loyalty to the regime rather than their legal expertise or impartiality. This ensures that the courts are populated with individuals predisposed to ruling in favor of the government, regardless of the merits of the case. Furthermore, authoritarian regimes may exert direct pressure on judges through intimidation, threats, or even fabricated charges to influence specific rulings. Budgetary constraints can also be weaponized, with funding for the judiciary slashed to limit its operational capacity and ability to effectively investigate government actions. Laws may be selectively interpreted or rewritten to legitimize actions that would otherwise be deemed illegal, further eroding the judiciary's ability to act as a check on power . The cumulative effect is a judiciary that is either unwilling or unable to challenge the regime, effectively turning it into a tool for enforcing the government's will.

The **press**, as the watchdog of society, is another key target for authoritarian regimes. A free and independent press plays a crucial role in informing the public, exposing corruption, and holding power accountable. Authoritarian regimes recognize the power of information and actively seek to control the narrative. Overt censorship is a common tactic, with newspapers, television stations, and online platforms subjected to strict regulations and monitoring. Journalists who dare to criticize the government face harassment, intimidation, arbitrary arrest, and even violence. More subtle methods of control include manipulating media ownership, granting preferential access to state-controlled media outlets, and spreading disinformation to discredit independent reporting. The internet, in particular, has become a battleground, with regimes employing sophisticated surveillance technologies and algorithms to monitor online activity, censor dissenting voices, and spread propaganda. By suppressing independent reporting and promoting state-controlled narratives, authoritarian regimes create an information environment that favors their rule and stifles critical thinking. The chilling effect of these actions leads to self-censorship, as journalists and media outlets become increasingly cautious about reporting on sensitive issues.

Civil society organizations (CSOs), which encompass a wide range of non-governmental organizations working on issues such as human rights, environmental protection, and social justice, also pose a threat to authoritarian regimes. CSOs empower citizens to organize, advocate for their rights, and hold the government accountable. Authoritarian regimes often view CSOs with suspicion, seeing them as potential sources of opposition and dissent. To weaken CSOs, regimes employ a range of tactics, including restrictive laws that limit their ability to register, operate, and receive funding. These laws often impose burdensome reporting requirements, grant the government broad powers to monitor CSO activities, and restrict their access to foreign funding. In some cases, regimes may even create their own government-organized non-governmental organizations (GONGOs) to mimic the activities of independent CSOs and co-opt public support. Activists and members of CSOs face surveillance, harassment, and arbitrary arrest. By constricting the space for civil society, authoritarian regimes silence dissenting voices and prevent citizens from organizing to challenge their rule.

The weakening of these independent institutions has profound consequences for society. Without a functioning judiciary, the rule of law is undermined, and citizens are left vulnerable to arbitrary and abusive actions by the state. Without a free press, the public is deprived of access to accurate information, making it difficult to hold the government accountable. Without a vibrant civil society, citizens are unable to organize and advocate for their rights, leading to a decline in civic engagement and participation. Ultimately, the erosion of independence creates a climate of fear and repression, where dissent is silenced, and individual freedoms are curtailed.

The systematic weakening of independent institutions is a hallmark of authoritarian rule. By undermining the judiciary, suppressing the press, and constricting civil society, authoritarian regimes seek to consolidate their power, stifle dissent, and maintain control over information. Understanding the mechanisms and consequences of this erosion is crucial for defending democratic values and promoting the development of societies where individual rights are protected, and governments are held accountable. The long-term effects of these actions can be devastating, leading to increased corruption, social unrest, and a decline in overall quality of life. Therefore, international efforts to support and strengthen independent institutions are essential for promoting democracy and human rights around the world.

THE EROSION OF DEMOCRACY
Gerrymandering, Voter Suppression, and the Manipulation of Elections

The health of a democracy rests on the principles of fair representation, equal access to the ballot box, and the integrity of the electoral process. However, these foundational pillars are increasingly threatened by a range of tactics designed to manipulate election outcomes and entrench the power of specific political interests. Among the most pervasive and damaging of these strategies are gerrymandering, voter suppression, and the broader manipulation of elections through various means. Analyzing these tactics reveals a disturbing trend: a concerted effort to undermine the will of the people and distort the democratic process.

GERRYMANDERING:
Distorting Representation Through Cartography

Gerrymandering, the practice of drawing electoral district boundaries to favor one political party or group over another, has a long and insidious history. Named after Elbridge Gerry, the Massachusetts governor who signed a bill in 1812 that created a salamander-shaped district to benefit his party, the practice has evolved into a sophisticated art of political mapmaking. The two primary techniques employed in gerrymandering are "cracking" and "packing." Cracking involves diluting the voting power of the opposing party by spreading its supporters across multiple districts, preventing them from forming a majority in any one. Packing, on the other hand, concentrates the opposing party's voters into a small number of districts, effectively wasting their votes in those districts while making surrounding districts more favorable to the party in power.

The consequences of gerrymandering are far-reaching. It can create safe seats for incumbents, leading to a lack of accountability and responsiveness to constituents. It can also result in a legislature that does not accurately reflect the political preferences of the population, leading to policies that are unpopular with the majority. For example, in states like North Carolina and Wisconsin, gerrymandered maps have consistently resulted in Republican control of the state legislature, even in years when Democrats have won a majority of the statewide vote. This disconnect between popular will and legislative outcome undermines the very essence of representative democracy. The legal challenges to gerrymandered maps often face significant hurdles, as courts grapple with defining what constitutes an unconstitutional partisan advantage and establishing clear standards for fair districting. Independent redistricting commissions, designed to remove partisan influence from the map-drawing process, represent a potential solution, but their implementation remains uneven across the country.

VOTER SUPPRESSION:
Erecting Barriers to the Ballot Box

Voter suppression encompasses a range of tactics designed to make it more difficult for certain groups of people to register and vote. These tactics disproportionately affect marginalized communities, including racial and ethnic minorities, low-income individuals, students, and the elderly. Common voter suppression strategies include:

Voter ID Laws: Requiring specific forms of identification to vote, often targeting IDs that are less accessible to low-income individuals and minorities. Strict photo ID laws, for instance, can disenfranchise those who lack access to transportation, birth certificates, or other required documents.

Purging Voter Rolls: Removing registered voters from the rolls for inactivity, often based on flawed data or infrequent address changes. Aggressive purges can disproportionately affect individuals who move frequently or who may not vote in every election.

Reducing Polling Places: Closing polling locations, particularly in minority neighborhoods and rural areas, leading to longer lines and increased travel distances. This can discourage participation, especially for those with limited transportation or mobility issues.

Restricting Early Voting and Absentee Voting: Limiting the availability of early voting periods and absentee ballots, making it more difficult for individuals with inflexible work schedules, disabilities, or other constraints to cast their votes.

Felony Disenfranchisement: Laws that prevent individuals with felony convictions from voting, even after they have completed their sentences. These laws disproportionately affect African Americans, contributing to significant racial disparities in voting rights.

The impact of voter suppression is profound. It not only disenfranchises eligible voters but also distorts the outcome of elections and undermines the legitimacy of the democratic process. Studies have shown that voter ID laws, for example, can significantly reduce turnout among minority voters. The fight against voter suppression requires constant vigilance and advocacy to ensure that all eligible citizens have equal access to the ballot box. The John Lewis Voting Rights Advancement Act, aimed at restoring key provisions of the Voting Rights Act of 1965, represents a crucial step in combating discriminatory voting practices, but its passage faces significant political obstacles.

BEYOND GERRYMANDERING AND VOTER SUPPRESSION
The Multifaceted Manipulation of Elections

While gerrymandering and voter suppression represent significant threats to democratic integrity, the manipulation of elections extends beyond these tactics. Other strategies employed to influence election outcomes include:

Disinformation Campaigns: Spreading false or misleading information to influence voter opinions and behavior. Social media platforms have become fertile ground for the dissemination of disinformation, making it increasingly difficult for voters to distinguish between credible sources and fabricated narratives.

Foreign Interference: Attempts by foreign governments to influence elections through hacking, propaganda, or other means. The 2016 US presidential election highlighted the vulnerability of democratic systems to foreign interference, raising concerns about the integrity of future elections.

Campaign Finance Abuses: The influence of money in politics can distort the electoral process, allowing wealthy donors and special interests to exert undue influence on political outcomes. Loopholes in campaign finance laws and the rise of super PACs have contributed to the increasing concentration of political power in the hands of a select few.

Challenges to Election Administration: Efforts to undermine public confidence in the integrity of election administration, often through baseless allegations of fraud or irregularities. These challenges can erode public trust in democratic institutions and sow the seeds of political instability.

Defending Democratic Integrity

Gerrymandering, voter suppression, and the broader manipulation of elections represent a grave threat to the health of democracy. These tactics undermine the principles of fair representation, equal access to the ballot box, and the integrity of the electoral process. Addressing these challenges requires a multi-pronged approach, including:

- **Legislative Reforms:** Enacting laws to combat gerrymandering, protect voting rights, and regulate campaign finance.

- **Judicial Action:** Challenging unconstitutional voting laws and ensuring fair districting practices.

- **Civic Education:** Promoting media literacy and critical thinking skills to combat disinformation and promote informed participation in the democratic process.

- **Voter Mobilization:** Encouraging voter registration and turnout, particularly among marginalized communities.

- **Protecting Election Officials and Workers:** Ensuring that election officials and workers are protected from intimidation and violence, and that they have the resources they need to conduct fair and secure elections.

The defense of democratic integrity requires constant vigilance and a commitment to upholding the principles of fairness, equality, and transparency in the electoral process. Only through sustained effort can we ensure that the will of the people is truly reflected in the outcome of elections and that democracy continues to thrive. The future of democracy depends on our willingness to confront these challenges head-on and safeguard the fundamental right to vote for all citizens.

CASE STUDIES:

United States (voter laws and institutional attacks), specific countries where checks and balances are dismantled

The health of a democracy hinges on the robust operation of its institutions and the effective enforcement of checks and balances. These mechanisms, designed to prevent the concentration of power and protect minority rights, are fundamental to ensuring accountability and preventing authoritarian drift. However, in recent years, democracies around the world have faced increasing threats from both internal and external forces seeking to undermine these vital safeguards. This essay will examine the erosion of democratic norms and institutions, focusing on specific case studies, including the United States and other nations where voter laws have been manipulated and institutional attacks have weakened the foundations of democratic governance. By analyzing these examples, we can gain a deeper understanding of the strategies employed to dismantle checks and balances and the potential consequences for democratic stability.

One particularly concerning example of democratic backsliding can be observed in the United States, where debates surrounding voter laws have intensified in recent years. Following the 2020 presidential election, numerous states, particularly those with Republican-controlled legislatures, enacted or attempted to enact laws that critics argue disproportionately restrict access to voting for minority groups, students, and the elderly. These measures include stricter voter ID requirements, limitations on early voting periods, reduced numbers of polling places in certain areas, and restrictions on mail-in voting. Proponents of these laws often claim they are necessary to prevent voter fraud and ensure election integrity. However, opponents contend that such justifications are often thinly veiled attempts to suppress voter turnout among demographic groups that tend to vote for the Democratic Party. The implementation of these laws raises serious concerns about the fundamental right to vote and the principle of equal access to the ballot box, which are cornerstones of a healthy democracy. The ongoing legal challenges to these laws highlight the deep partisan divisions surrounding voting rights and the fragility of democratic norms in the face of political polarization.

Beyond voter laws, the United States has also witnessed instances that can be characterized as institutional attacks. The January 6th, 2021, attack on the U.S. Capitol, fueled by unsubstantiated claims of widespread voter fraud, represents a stark example of the potential for political violence to disrupt the democratic process. The attack, aimed at preventing the certification of the presidential election results, not only threatened the physical safety of lawmakers but also undermined the peaceful transfer of power, a bedrock principle of American democracy. Furthermore, the politicization of judicial appointments, particularly at the Supreme Court level, has raised concerns about the independence and impartiality of the judiciary. Accusations of partisan bias in judicial decision-making, coupled with efforts to pack the courts with ideologically aligned judges, can erode public trust in the judiciary as a neutral arbiter of justice. The cumulative effect of these actions – restrictive voter laws, attacks on democratic institutions, and the politicization of the judiciary – poses a significant challenge to the resilience of American democracy.

To further illustrate the global nature of this challenge, it is crucial to examine instances of democratic backsliding in other countries where checks and balances have been dismantled. In Hungary, for example, the government of Viktor Orbán has been accused of systematically weakening independent institutions, including the judiciary, the media, and civil society organizations. Through a combination of legislative changes and political pressure, the government has consolidated its control over these key sectors, effectively silencing dissenting voices and limiting the ability of opposition parties to challenge its authority. Similarly, in Poland, the ruling Law and Justice party has taken steps to undermine the independence of the judiciary, leading to concerns about the rule of law and the separation of powers. These actions have drawn criticism from the European Union and international human rights organizations, who argue that they violate fundamental democratic principles.

Turkey under Recep Tayyip Erdoğan provides another compelling case study. Following a failed coup attempt in 2016, the government initiated a widespread crackdown on dissent, arresting journalists, academics, and political opponents. The government has also exerted increasing control over the media and the judiciary, further eroding checks and balances and limiting the space for independent voices. Constitutional changes that granted the president greater executive powers have further solidified Erdoğan's grip on power and weakened the role of parliament. These examples from Hungary, Poland, and Turkey highlight the diverse strategies employed by authoritarian-leaning governments to dismantle checks and balances and consolidate power.

The consequences of dismantling checks and balances can be far-reaching and detrimental to democratic stability. When independent institutions are weakened, corruption can flourish, human rights can be violated with impunity, and the voices of marginalized groups can be silenced. The erosion of democratic norms can also lead to political instability, social unrest, and even violent conflict. Furthermore, the decline of democracy in one country can have ripple effects on the broader global order, emboldening authoritarian regimes and undermining international efforts to promote human rights and democratic governance.

In conclusion, the erosion of democracy is a complex and multifaceted phenomenon that requires careful analysis and proactive responses. The case studies of the United States, Hungary, Poland, and Turkey demonstrate the diverse strategies employed to dismantle checks and balances, ranging from restrictive voter laws to attacks on independent institutions and the politicization of the judiciary. To safeguard democracy, it is essential to strengthen independent institutions, protect voting rights, promote media pluralism, and foster a culture of respect for the rule of law. International cooperation and vigilance are also crucial to holding governments accountable for their actions and supporting civil society organizations working to promote democracy and human rights around the world. The future of democracy depends on our collective commitment to defending its principles and resisting the forces that seek to undermine it.

HUMAN RIGHTS UNDER SIEGE
The Price of Power

Authoritarian regimes, in their relentless pursuit of control and consolidation of power, pose a significant and enduring threat to human rights. A core tactic employed in this pursuit is the systematic weakening, and often outright dismantling, of independent institutions that serve as bulwarks against unchecked authority. These institutions, including the judiciary, the press, and civil society organizations, are essential for upholding the rule of law, fostering accountability, and protecting the fundamental rights of citizens. By targeting these pillars of a free and just society, authoritarian regimes create an environment where human rights are not only vulnerable but actively suppressed, paving the way for abuses to occur with impunity.

The judiciary, in a functioning democratic society, serves as an impartial arbiter of disputes and a guardian of constitutional rights. An independent judiciary is empowered to review government actions, ensure that laws are applied fairly, and hold state actors accountable for violations of the law. However, authoritarian regimes actively undermine this independence through various means. They may appoint loyalists to judicial positions, often prioritizing political allegiance over legal expertise and integrity. Judges who dare to rule against the regime face intimidation, harassment, and even removal from office. Laws may be selectively enforced, with critics of the government bearing the brunt of judicial scrutiny while those aligned with the regime enjoy preferential treatment. Further, the structure of the legal system itself might be manipulated, with special courts established to handle politically sensitive cases outside the purview of normal legal procedures, further eroding the independence of the judiciary. By effectively neutering the judicial system, authoritarian regimes ensure that they operate outside the bounds of law, shielding themselves from accountability and denying citizens recourse against state abuses.

A free and vibrant press acts as a crucial watchdog, scrutinizing government actions, exposing corruption, and informing the public about matters of public interest. This role is diametrically opposed to the objectives of authoritarian regimes, which seek to control the narrative and suppress dissent. Consequently, the independent press becomes a primary target. Authoritarian regimes employ a range of tactics to silence critical voices, including censorship, the imposition of restrictive licensing requirements, and the harassment and arrest of journalists. State-controlled media outlets are weaponized to disseminate propaganda, demonize critics, and create a distorted picture of reality. Online spaces, which once offered a platform for independent expression, are increasingly subject to surveillance and censorship, with governments employing sophisticated technologies to monitor online activity and silence dissenting voices. Laws against defamation and "spreading false information" are often weaponized to silence journalists who report critically on the government, creating a chilling effect that discourages investigative journalism and limits the free flow of information. By controlling the flow of information, authoritarian regimes can manipulate public opinion, suppress dissent, and maintain a tight grip on power.

Civil society organizations (CSOs), including human rights groups, advocacy organizations, and community-based initiatives, play a vital role in promoting human rights, holding governments accountable, and providing essential services to marginalized populations. These organizations act as a crucial link between citizens and the state, amplifying the voices of the vulnerable and advocating for policy changes that promote justice and equality. However, authoritarian regimes view CSOs as a potential threat to their authority, particularly when they focus on issues such as human rights, democracy, and good governance. As such, they often implement restrictive laws that limit the ability of CSOs to operate effectively. These laws may require CSOs to register with the government, subject them to burdensome reporting requirements, and restrict their access to funding, particularly from foreign sources. CSOs that challenge the government's policies or expose human rights abuses face harassment, intimidation, and even closure. Activists and human rights defenders are often targeted with surveillance, arbitrary arrest, and politically motivated prosecutions. By constricting the space for civil society, authoritarian regimes silence critical voices, prevent independent monitoring of human rights violations, and weaken the ability of citizens to organize and advocate for change, furthering the erosion of fundamental freedoms.

The systematic weakening of independent institutions is a hallmark of authoritarian rule, a calculated strategy designed to consolidate power, suppress dissent, and shield the regime from accountability. The consequences for human rights are devastating. Without an independent judiciary, the rule of law collapses, and citizens are left vulnerable to arbitrary state actions. Without a free press, the public is deprived of access to accurate information, and abuses of power remain hidden. Without a vibrant civil society, the voices of the marginalized are silenced, and the ability to advocate for change is curtailed. The combined effect is a climate of fear and repression, where human rights are routinely violated with impunity, and the promise of a just and equitable society remains an unfulfilled aspiration. The erosion of these vital institutions serves as a stark reminder of the precariousness of human rights under authoritarian rule and the constant need for vigilance in defending them. The international community must actively support the resilience of these institutions in the face of authoritarian pressure, bolstering their capacity to function independently and hold power accountable, ultimately contributing to the advancement of human rights worldwide.

THE CASUALTIES OF "PROGRESS"
Dismantling Safety Nets and the Environment

Let's examine how authoritarian regimes prioritize economic growth over human rights and environmental protection.

The relentless pursuit of "progress," often defined in narrow economic terms, can become a dangerous ideology, particularly when wielded by authoritarian regimes. These regimes, prioritizing rapid economic growth above all else, frequently dismantle crucial safety nets and disregard environmental protection, leaving a trail of human suffering and ecological devastation in their wake. This essay will explore how the single-minded focus on economic expansion under authoritarian rule systematically undermines human rights and environmental sustainability, ultimately revealing the devastating human and ecological costs disguised as "progress."

One of the most glaring casualties of this distorted vision of progress is the erosion of social safety nets. Authoritarian regimes, often seeking to attract foreign investment and project an image of economic efficiency, frequently cut back on social programs such as healthcare, education, and unemployment benefits. This dismantling of the welfare state is often justified under the guise of fiscal responsibility, efficiency, or the claim that these programs create dependency. However, the reality on the ground is far grimmer. Without adequate social safety nets, vulnerable populations are left exposed to economic shocks, natural disasters, and health crises. The lack of affordable healthcare can lead to preventable illnesses and premature death, while inadequate education opportunities perpetuate cycles of poverty and limit social mobility. The absence of unemployment benefits throws families into destitution, forcing them to make desperate choices to survive. Critics are often silenced, labeled as enemies of progress or saboteurs of the economic plan, further solidifying the regime's control and hindering any meaningful opposition to these damaging policies. The human cost of prioritizing economic growth over social well-being is immeasurable, resulting in increased inequality, social unrest, and diminished quality of life for a significant portion of the population.

Furthermore, the environment becomes a prime target in the relentless pursuit of economic growth. Authoritarian regimes often prioritize resource extraction and industrial development, regardless of the environmental consequences. Regulations designed to protect air and water quality, conserve natural resources, and preserve biodiversity are often weakened or ignored altogether, paving the way for unchecked pollution and environmental degradation. Forests are cleared for agriculture and logging, rivers are dammed for hydroelectric power, and mines are dug with little regard for the surrounding ecosystems. This environmental destruction not only threatens biodiversity and disrupts ecological balance but also has direct and devastating consequences for human health. Air and water pollution can lead to respiratory illnesses, cancer, and other health problems. Deforestation can contribute to climate change, increasing the frequency and intensity of extreme weather events such as floods, droughts, and heatwaves, which disproportionately affect the poor and vulnerable. The long-term effects of environmental damage can be irreversible, jeopardizing the health and well-being of future generations. For instance, the Aral Sea disaster, largely driven by Soviet-era agricultural policies focused on cotton production, serves as a stark example of how prioritizing economic output over environmental sustainability can lead to ecological collapse and widespread human suffering.

The justification for this exploitation of natural resources and dismantling of environmental protections often rests on the argument that these are necessary sacrifices for economic development. Authoritarian regimes often claim that environmental concerns are a luxury that developing countries cannot afford, arguing that rapid economic growth is the only way to lift their populations out of poverty. However, this argument is deeply flawed. Sustainable development, which balances economic growth with environmental protection and social equity, offers a far more viable and equitable path to prosperity. By investing in clean energy, promoting sustainable agriculture, and protecting natural resources, countries can achieve economic growth without sacrificing the health and well-being of their citizens or jeopardizing the environment for future generations.

Moreover, the lack of transparency and accountability inherent in authoritarian regimes exacerbates the problem. Without a free press, independent judiciary, and vibrant civil society, there are few checks on the power of the state and its allies. Corruption flourishes, leading to the prioritization of private gain over public good. Environmental regulations are often selectively enforced, protecting powerful interests while punishing ordinary citizens. Whistleblowers and activists who dare to speak out against environmental abuses are often silenced, intimidated, or even imprisoned. This lack of accountability creates a climate of impunity, encouraging further environmental destruction and undermining efforts to promote sustainable development.

In conclusion, the relentless pursuit of economic growth under authoritarian regimes often comes at a terrible cost. By dismantling social safety nets and disregarding environmental protection, these regimes prioritize short-term economic gains over long-term human well-being and ecological sustainability. The resulting inequality, social unrest, and environmental degradation undermine the very foundations of a prosperous and just society. True progress requires a more holistic and equitable approach, one that prioritizes the health, well-being, and rights of all citizens, while also protecting the environment for future generations. Only then can we hope to create a truly sustainable and prosperous future for all. The illusion of progress peddled by authoritarian regimes must be exposed for what it is: a Faustian bargain that sacrifices the welfare of the many for the enrichment of the few, leaving behind a legacy of broken promises and a ravaged planet.

Let's analyze the consequences of deregulation, privatization, and the exploitation of natural resources.

The relentless march often labeled "progress" is rarely a uniform advance for all. While proponents tout the economic efficiencies and innovative potential unleashed by deregulation, privatization, and the exploitation of natural resources, a closer examination reveals a trail of casualties left in their wake. This essay will delve into the multifaceted consequences of these policies, arguing that the pursuit of unchecked economic growth, often divorced from social and environmental considerations, leads to significant and often irreversible damage to communities, ecosystems, and the very fabric of societal well-being.

Deregulation, frequently presented as a means of freeing markets and fostering competition, can quickly morph into a race to the bottom. When environmental protections, labor standards, and consumer safety regulations are weakened or dismantled, the immediate beneficiaries are often corporations seeking to maximize profits. However, the long-term costs are borne by the public. Consider the deregulation of the financial industry in the lead-up to the 2008 financial crisis. The relaxation of oversight allowed for increasingly risky and speculative ventures, ultimately culminating in a global economic meltdown that devastated livelihoods, eroded trust in institutions, and necessitated massive public bailouts. Similarly, the deregulation of environmental regulations can lead to increased pollution, habitat destruction, and public health crises, as companies prioritize short-term gains over the long-term sustainability of the environment. The Flint water crisis, a direct consequence of cost-cutting measures and inadequate regulatory oversight, serves as a stark reminder of the human cost of prioritizing profit over public safety.

Privatization, the transfer of public services and assets to private ownership, is often promoted as a way to improve efficiency and reduce government spending. However, the profit motive inherent in private enterprise can fundamentally alter the provision of essential services. When healthcare, education, or utilities are privatized, access can become contingent on ability to pay, exacerbating existing inequalities and creating new barriers for vulnerable populations. The focus shifts from serving the public good to maximizing shareholder value, potentially leading to compromised quality, reduced accessibility, and increased costs for consumers. For example, the privatization of water systems has, in some cases, resulted in higher prices, neglected infrastructure, and even water shutoffs for low-income residents. The argument that private companies are inherently more efficient often ignores the fact that public services are often designed to serve everyone, regardless of their ability to pay, while private companies are primarily accountable to their shareholders.

The exploitation of natural resources, while undeniably a driver of economic growth, carries profound environmental and social consequences. The extraction of fossil fuels, minerals, and timber often leads to deforestation, habitat loss, water contamination, and air pollution. These environmental impacts disproportionately affect marginalized communities, who often live in close proximity to extraction sites and lack the resources to mitigate the negative effects. Furthermore, the pursuit of natural resources can fuel conflict and displacement, as powerful corporations and governments seek to control access to valuable resources, often at the expense of local populations. The Niger Delta, for instance, has suffered decades of environmental degradation and social unrest as a result of oil extraction, highlighting the devastating consequences of prioritizing profit over the well-being of communities and the environment.

Moreover, the relentless pursuit of economic growth, fueled by these policies, often overlooks the importance of social cohesion, community well-being, and environmental sustainability. The focus on GDP as the primary measure of progress fails to capture the true cost of environmental damage, social inequality, and the erosion of cultural values. Alternative measures of progress, such as the Genuine Progress

Indicator (GPI), attempt to account for these factors, providing a more comprehensive picture of societal well-being.

While deregulation, privatization, and the exploitation of natural resources may generate short-term economic benefits, their long-term consequences are often detrimental to communities, ecosystems, and the overall health of society. A truly progressive approach requires a fundamental shift in priorities, one that prioritizes social and environmental well-being alongside economic growth. This necessitates strengthening regulations, ensuring equitable access to essential services, and adopting sustainable practices that protect our planet for future generations. Only then can we ensure that the pursuit of "progress" benefits all, rather than leaving a trail of casualties in its wake. This requires critical evaluation, proactive policies focused on sustainability and equity, and a willingness to reconsider the very definition of "progress" that guides our actions.

CASE STUDIES:

Environmental destruction in the Amazon, exploitation of workers in developing countries.

THE INTERTWINED EVILS
Environmental Destruction in the Amazon and Labor Exploitation in the Developing World

The relentless pursuit of economic growth, often fueled by insatiable consumer demand in developed nations, has cast a long shadow over the developing world. Two of the most devastating consequences of this dynamic are the rampant environmental destruction occurring in vital ecosystems like the Amazon rainforest, and the widespread exploitation of workers in developing countries, often driven by the same underlying forces of globalization and profit maximization. While seemingly disparate issues, these crises are inextricably linked, forming a complex web of interconnected problems that demand urgent and multifaceted solutions.

The Amazon rainforest, often referred to as the "lungs of the planet," plays a crucial role in regulating global climate patterns, absorbing vast quantities of carbon dioxide, and generating oxygen. However, this vital ecosystem is under siege. Deforestation, driven primarily by agricultural expansion (particularly cattle ranching and soy cultivation), illegal logging, and mining activities, is occurring at an alarming rate. The consequences are far-reaching, extending beyond the immediate loss of biodiversity and habitat. Deforestation contributes significantly to greenhouse gas emissions, exacerbates climate change, disrupts regional weather patterns, and threatens the livelihoods of indigenous communities who depend on the forest for their survival. The short-term economic gains derived from these destructive activities are dwarfed by the long-term ecological and social costs. The pursuit of cheap land for agriculture, driven by global demand for commodities, fuels a cycle of destruction that undermines the very foundations of a sustainable future.

Simultaneously, in many developing nations, workers face exploitative labor practices that rob them of their dignity, health, and fair compensation. Driven by the pressure to produce goods at the lowest possible cost, multinational corporations and local businesses alike often engage in practices such as paying poverty wages, imposing unsafe working conditions, denying workers basic rights to organize and bargain collectively, and employing child labor. Garment factories in Bangladesh, cobalt mines in the Democratic Republic of Congo, and agricultural plantations in Southeast Asia are just a few examples of locations where workers are routinely subjected to these abuses. The demand for cheap consumer goods in developed countries fuels this race to the bottom, incentivizing businesses to cut corners and exploit vulnerable workers.

The link between environmental destruction and labor exploitation becomes clearer when we consider the underlying drivers. Both are often symptoms of a global economic system that prioritizes profit above all else. The same forces that drive deforestation in the Amazon – the demand for cheap land and resources – also incentivize the exploitation of workers in developing countries who are tasked with producing the commodities that are extracted from the land. For instance, mining operations, whether legal or illegal, not only devastate the environment but also often rely on exploitative labor practices, including forced labor and child labor. Similarly, the expansion of agriculture often leads to the displacement of local communities and the creation of a vulnerable workforce that is susceptible to exploitation.

Additionally, weak governance and corruption in many developing countries exacerbate both problems. Inadequate environmental regulations and lax enforcement allow companies to engage in destructive activities with impunity. Similarly, weak labor laws and a lack of effective enforcement mechanisms enable employers to exploit workers without fear of consequences. This creates a vicious cycle in which environmental destruction and labor exploitation reinforce each other, perpetuating poverty and inequality.

Addressing these intertwined evils requires a multifaceted approach that tackles the root causes of the problem. This includes:

- **Strengthening environmental regulations and enforcement:** Governments in developing countries must enact and enforce robust environmental regulations to protect vital ecosystems like the Amazon. This includes cracking down on illegal logging, mining, and agricultural expansion, and investing in sustainable land management practices.

- o **Promoting fair labor standards:** Governments must also strengthen labor laws and enforcement mechanisms to ensure that workers are paid fair wages, provided with safe working conditions, and allowed to exercise their rights to organize and bargain collectively.

- o **Combating corruption:** Tackling corruption is essential to ensuring that environmental and labor regulations are effectively enforced. This requires strengthening institutions, promoting transparency, and holding corrupt officials accountable.

- o **Promoting sustainable consumption:** Consumers in developed countries must be aware of the impact of their purchasing decisions on the environment and workers in developing countries. Supporting companies that adhere to fair labor practices and sustainable environmental practices can help to create a more just and sustainable global economy.

- o **Empowering local communities:** Indigenous communities and local organizations play a crucial role in protecting the environment and advocating for the rights of workers. Supporting these communities and organizations can help to ensure that development is sustainable and equitable.

- o **International Cooperation:** Developed nations have a responsibility to assist developing countries in their efforts to protect the environment and promote fair labor standards. This includes providing financial and technical assistance, as well as promoting responsible investment practices.

The environmental destruction in the Amazon and the exploitation of workers in developing countries are not isolated problems. They are interconnected symptoms of a global economic system that prioritizes profit over people and the planet. Addressing these intertwined evils requires a fundamental shift in our values and priorities, as well as a commitment to building a more just and sustainable global economy. Only through collective action and a commitment to ethical and responsible practices can we hope to protect our planet and ensure a decent standard of living for all.

SILENCING THE VOICES
Suppressing Freedom of Expression and Assembly

Freedom of expression and assembly are cornerstones of a democratic society, allowing for the robust exchange of ideas, the peaceful articulation of grievances, and the collective pursuit of societal betterment. These fundamental rights, enshrined in international human rights declarations and national constitutions around the world, are essential for holding power accountable and fostering a vibrant, engaged citizenry. However, throughout history and across diverse political landscapes, these freedoms have been consistently and systematically suppressed, often with devastating consequences. Understanding the mechanisms and motivations behind this suppression is crucial to safeguarding these vital rights and ensuring a more just and equitable world.

The suppression of freedom of expression and assembly manifests in a variety of forms, ranging from overt censorship and violent crackdowns to more subtle forms of manipulation and intimidation. Historically, autocratic regimes have relied on strict control of the media, banning dissenting publications, and imprisoning journalists who dared to challenge the status quo. The printing press, once hailed as a revolutionary tool for disseminating knowledge, was quickly targeted by authorities seeking to maintain their grip on power. Similarly, the right to assemble was often curtailed through the banning of protests, the use of excessive force against demonstrators, and the implementation of restrictive laws that made it virtually impossible to organize public gatherings. Examples abound throughout history, from the suppression of revolutionary ideas in pre-revolutionary France to the brutal crackdowns on student protests in Tiananmen Square.

Beyond outright bans and violence, more insidious methods of suppression are employed. These include disinformation campaigns designed to discredit dissenting voices, the use of surveillance technologies to monitor and intimidate activists, and the manipulation of legal frameworks to silence critics. Strategic Lawsuits Against Public Participation (SLAPPs), for example, are often used to financially and emotionally exhaust individuals who speak out against powerful corporations or government actors. Online platforms, while offering unprecedented opportunities for expression, have also become battlegrounds for censorship and manipulation. Algorithms can be used to silence certain voices, while coordinated disinformation campaigns can drown out legitimate opinions. The rise of online surveillance also chills free speech, as individuals may be hesitant to express themselves freely knowing that their online activities are being monitored.

The motivations behind suppressing freedom of expression and assembly are often complex and intertwined. In many cases, the primary goal is to maintain the power and privilege of those in authority. By silencing dissent, regimes can prevent challenges to their legitimacy and suppress calls for reform. Fear of instability and social unrest can also drive suppression, as authorities may believe that restricting freedom of expression is necessary to maintain order. Economic interests also play a significant role, as powerful corporations and industries may seek to silence critics who expose their harmful practices or advocate for regulations that would impact their profits. Furthermore, ideological extremism, whether religious, political, or cultural, can lead to the suppression of dissenting views in the name of protecting a particular worldview.

The consequences of suppressing freedom of expression and assembly are far-reaching and devastating. On an individual level, it leads to self-censorship, fear, and a sense of disempowerment. When individuals are afraid to speak their minds or participate in public discourse, they are denied the opportunity to contribute to the shaping of their own societies. On a societal level, the suppression of these freedoms leads to a decline in critical thinking, a narrowing of perspectives, and a weakening of democratic institutions. Without the ability to openly debate and challenge ideas, societies become stagnant and vulnerable to corruption and abuse of power. Furthermore, suppressed grievances can eventually erupt into violent conflict, as people feel they have no other recourse to address their concerns.

Combating the suppression of freedom of expression and assembly requires a multi-pronged approach. First and foremost, it is essential to uphold and strengthen legal protections for these rights, both domestically and internationally. This includes ensuring that laws relating to speech and assembly are clear, narrowly tailored, and do not disproportionately restrict these freedoms. Secondly, it is crucial to promote media literacy and critical thinking skills, enabling individuals to discern between credible information and disinformation. Thirdly, supporting independent journalism and civil society organizations that advocate for freedom of expression is essential. These organizations play a vital role in monitoring human rights abuses, providing legal assistance to victims, and raising awareness about the importance of these freedoms. Finally, international pressure and sanctions can be used to hold accountable regimes that systematically violate freedom of expression and assembly.

In conclusion, the suppression of freedom of expression and assembly is a persistent threat to democratic values and human rights. It takes many forms, driven by a variety of motivations, and has devastating consequences for individuals and societies alike. By understanding the mechanisms of suppression, strengthening legal protections, promoting media literacy, and supporting independent journalism and civil society organizations, we can safeguard these vital freedoms and create a more just and equitable world where all voices can be heard. The fight for freedom of expression and assembly is a constant struggle, but it is a struggle worth fighting, for the sake of democracy, justice, and the future of humanity.

Let's examine the crackdown on dissent, the persecution of journalists and activists, and the suppression of free speech.

The erosion of democratic values in many parts of the world is increasingly characterized by a systematic crackdown on dissent, the persecution of journalists and activists, and the suppression of free speech. These interconnected trends represent a grave threat to human rights, accountable governance, and the very fabric of open societies. Examining these phenomena reveals a complex and multifaceted challenge, requiring a nuanced understanding of their causes, consequences, and potential solutions.

The suppression of dissent often begins with the demonization of critical voices. Governments and powerful actors, seeking to maintain their authority and control, frequently label dissenting opinions as "fake news," "foreign interference," or even "terrorism." This rhetoric serves to delegitimize opposition, justify restrictive measures, and cultivate a climate of fear that discourages individuals from expressing their concerns. Laws ostensibly designed to combat terrorism or maintain national security are often weaponized to silence political opponents, human rights defenders, and anyone who dares to challenge the status quo. Examples of this can be found in countries where vaguely worded "anti-terrorism" legislation is used to prosecute peaceful protestors or journalists reporting on sensitive issues.

Journalists and activists, who play a crucial role in holding power accountable and informing the public, are often targeted with particular ferocity. They face a range of threats, including physical violence, arbitrary arrest, online harassment, and smear campaigns. Investigative journalists who uncover corruption or expose human rights abuses are especially vulnerable, as their work often directly challenges the interests of those in power. The persecution of journalists can take many forms, from the outright assassination of dissidents to the more subtle but equally damaging practice of restricting access to information, censoring media outlets, and imposing exorbitant fines for critical reporting. The chilling effect of such actions extends beyond the immediate victims, deterring other journalists from pursuing similar investigations and further limiting the flow of information to the public.

The suppression of free speech manifests in a variety of ways, both online and offline. Governments often employ sophisticated surveillance technologies to monitor citizens' communications, track their movements, and identify potential dissidents. Online censorship, ranging from blocking websites and social media platforms to manipulating search engine results, is becoming increasingly common. These tactics are particularly effective in stifling dissent in authoritarian regimes, where the internet is often the only remaining space for independent expression. Even in countries with more established democratic traditions, concerns are growing about the potential for social media platforms to be used to spread disinformation and manipulate public opinion, leading to calls for greater regulation and accountability.

The consequences of this crackdown are far-reaching. When dissent is stifled, corruption flourishes, human rights abuses go unchecked, and political instability increases. The erosion of trust in institutions and the rise of polarization can further exacerbate these problems, creating a vicious cycle of repression and unrest. Furthermore, the suppression of free speech stifles innovation, creativity, and economic progress. When individuals are afraid to express their ideas or challenge conventional wisdom, societies become stagnant and less resilient to change.

Combating the crackdown on dissent requires a multifaceted approach that addresses both the symptoms and the underlying causes. This includes:

- o **Strengthening legal protections for freedom of expression and association:** This requires ensuring that laws are clearly defined, narrowly tailored, and consistent with international human rights standards.

- o **Promoting media freedom and independence:** This includes protecting journalists from violence and harassment, ensuring access to information, and fostering a diverse and pluralistic media landscape.

- o **Supporting civil society organizations:** These organizations play a crucial role in monitoring human rights abuses, advocating for policy changes, and providing legal assistance to victims.

- o **Holding governments accountable for human rights violations:** This requires international pressure, sanctions, and other measures to deter repressive behavior.

- o **Promoting digital literacy and media literacy:** This helps individuals to critically evaluate information and resist manipulation.

- o **Working with technology companies to ensure that their platforms are not used to suppress dissent or spread disinformation.** The fight for freedom of expression and against the suppression of dissent is a global imperative. By understanding the complex dynamics at play and working together to promote human rights and democratic values, we can help to create a more just and equitable world for all. The silence of dissent is the breeding ground for tyranny, and the unwavering pursuit of truth and open dialogue is the cornerstone of a truly free society.

Let's analyze the use of censorship, intimidation, and violence to silence opposition.

To fully understand the mechanisms of authoritarian control, it's crucial to analyze how regimes utilize censorship, intimidation, and violence as tools to silence opposition. These tactics, often intertwined and mutually reinforcing, aim to create a climate of fear, suppress dissent, and maintain the ruling power's grip on information and narrative. Each plays a distinct role in dismantling the foundations of a free and open society.

Censorship, in its various forms, acts as the first line of defense against dissenting voices. It's the systematic suppression of information, ideas, and artistic expression deemed threatening to the ruling power. This can manifest as direct control over media outlets, requiring government approval for publications, radio broadcasts, and television programs. It can also take the form of online censorship, where websites are blocked, social media posts are removed, and algorithms are manipulated to downrank or shadow ban dissenting views. Beyond direct control, censorship can be more insidious, relying on self-censorship born out of fear of reprisal. Journalists and artists, understanding the potential consequences of challenging the regime, may preemptively moderate their work, leading to a chilling effect on independent thought and creative expression. The absence of diverse perspectives creates an echo chamber, reinforcing the official narrative and hindering critical thinking.

Intimidation follows censorship, serving as a constant reminder of the consequences of defiance. This tactic aims to instill fear and discourage individuals from expressing opposition, organizing protests, or even engaging in private conversations critical of the regime. Intimidation can take many forms, from overt surveillance and harassment of activists and journalists to subtle threats directed at family members. Public shaming campaigns, often orchestrated through state-controlled media, can be used to discredit and isolate individuals who dare to speak out. Furthermore, the selective enforcement of laws, where legitimate activities are criminalized or punished disproportionately, serves to create an atmosphere of uncertainty and vulnerability. The constant threat of arbitrary arrest, detention, or economic hardship silences potential dissidents and discourages others from following in their footsteps.

Finally, when censorship and intimidation fail to completely suppress opposition, violence stands as the ultimate weapon. It's the blunt instrument of authoritarian control, used to eliminate threats and instill widespread terror. Violence can range from police brutality during protests to targeted assassinations of prominent dissidents. Arbitrary arrests, torture in prisons, and extrajudicial killings are all part of the spectrum of violence employed to silence opposition. The brutality is often public and visible, designed to send a clear message to anyone contemplating resistance. Furthermore, the state may employ paramilitaries or gangs to carry out acts of violence with a degree of plausible deniability, further blurring the lines of accountability and creating a climate of pervasive fear. The threat of violence, even when not explicitly enacted, serves as a powerful deterrent to dissent, forcing individuals to prioritize their safety and security above their right to free expression.

Censorship, intimidation, and violence form a triad of oppression, each reinforcing the others to create a suffocating environment where dissent is stifled and individual freedoms are suppressed. By controlling the flow of information, creating a climate of fear, and resorting to physical violence when necessary, authoritarian regimes maintain their grip on power and crush any potential challenges to their authority. Understanding the interplay of these tactics is crucial for recognizing and resisting authoritarianism in its various manifestations. Furthermore, safeguarding independent media, protecting human rights defenders, and promoting the rule of law are essential steps in countering these oppressive strategies and building societies where freedom of thought and expression can flourish.

CASE STUDIES:

Dissidents in Belarus, journalists murdered in Mexico, Hong Kong's pro-democracy movement.

Dissidents in Belarus, journalists murdered in Mexico, Hong Kong's pro-democracy movement. These seemingly disparate examples, scattered across continents and manifesting in diverse political landscapes, are united by a common thread: the suppression of fundamental freedoms and the often-deadly consequences faced by those who dare to challenge authoritarianism and injustice. They serve as stark reminders that the struggle for human rights, far from being a settled victory, remains a constant and often perilous endeavor.

In Belarus, the iron fist of Alexander Lukashenko has been met with unwavering resistance from a population yearning for democratic governance. Following the disputed 2020 presidential election, peaceful protests were met with brutal force, mass arrests, and systematic torture. Dissidents, activists, and ordinary citizens who voiced opposition to the regime have been imprisoned, exiled, or silenced through intimidation. The courageous defiance of the Belarusian people, despite the immense personal risks involved, underscores the enduring human desire for self-determination and the right to choose one's own leaders. The international community has largely condemned the actions of the

Lukashenko regime, yet the struggle for democracy within Belarus continues, fueled by the unwavering spirit of its people.

The situation in Mexico presents a different, yet equally troubling, manifestation of the suppression of freedom. Here, it is not necessarily the state itself that is directly responsible for curtailing rights, but rather the pervasive power of organized crime. Journalists, particularly those investigating drug cartels and government corruption, face an alarmingly high risk of violence and assassination. The murders of reporters like Javier Valdez Cárdenas and Regina Martínez Pérez, among countless others, highlight the deadly consequences of challenging powerful vested interests. The impunity surrounding these crimes not only silences critical voices but also erodes public trust in institutions and undermines the rule of law, fostering a climate of fear and self-censorship. The lack of effective protection for journalists in Mexico raises serious questions about the government's ability and willingness to safeguard freedom of the press and hold perpetrators accountable.

Hong Kong's pro-democracy movement, once a vibrant symbol of resistance against encroaching Chinese influence, has been systematically dismantled in recent years. The imposition of the National Security Law in 2020 effectively criminalized dissent, silencing opposition voices and curtailing fundamental freedoms of speech, assembly, and the press. Leading pro-democracy figures have been imprisoned, exiled, or forced into silence. The vibrant civil society that once characterized Hong Kong has been replaced by an atmosphere of fear and self-censorship. The erosion of Hong Kong's autonomy serves as a cautionary tale about the fragility of democratic institutions and the willingness of authoritarian regimes to suppress dissent in the name of national security. The crackdown on Hong Kong's pro-democracy movement sends a chilling message to other regions grappling with authoritarian tendencies, underscoring the importance of international solidarity in defending democratic values.

These examples, while geographically diverse, represent a global struggle for fundamental human rights. They underscore the crucial importance of supporting dissidents, protecting journalists, and advocating for democratic principles around the world. The fight for freedom is not merely a political ideal; it is a fundamental human imperative that demands our constant vigilance and unwavering support. Only through sustained international pressure, robust advocacy, and unwavering solidarity with those on the front lines of this struggle can we hope to create a world where human rights are respected and protected for all.

THE EROSION OF JUSTICE
Undermining the Rule of Law

The foundation of any just and stable society rests upon the principle of the Rule of Law. When this foundation weakens, the edifice of social order begins to crack, threatening the very fabric of communal existence. The erosion of the Rule of Law, through corruption, inequality, and weak enforcement, is not merely a legal problem; it is a societal crisis that demands immediate and comprehensive attention.

The Rule of Law, in its essence, is the principle that all individuals and institutions, both public and private, are subject to and accountable under the law. It is a system where laws are publicly promulgated, equally enforced, and independently adjudicated. It is a cornerstone of democratic governance and a prerequisite for sustainable development. Crucially, the Rule of Law is not simply about having laws in place; it is about the quality, fairness, and accessibility of those laws, and the impartial application of those laws to all. It is the antithesis of arbitrary power and the guarantor of individual liberties.

At its core, the Rule of Law is underpinned by several fundamental principles. First, **equality before the law** dictates that all individuals, regardless of their wealth, status, or influence, are treated equally under the legal system. No one is above the law, and everyone is entitled to the same legal protections and opportunities. Second, the **accountability of government officials** ensures that those in positions of power are held responsible for their actions and are subject to legal scrutiny. This prevents abuse of authority and promotes good governance. Third, **transparency in legal processes** requires that legal proceedings are open, accessible, and understandable to the public. This fosters trust in the system and reduces the potential for corruption or undue influence. Finally, the **protection of fundamental rights** guarantees the inherent rights and freedoms of all individuals, including the right to a fair trial, freedom of expression, and protection from arbitrary arrest and detention.

These principles are essential for a just and stable society because they provide a framework for resolving disputes peacefully, protecting individual liberties, and promoting economic development. When the Rule of Law is upheld, individuals are more likely to invest in their communities, businesses are more likely to thrive, and societies are more likely to prosper. Conversely, when the Rule of Law is undermined, societies become vulnerable to instability, conflict, and economic stagnation.

One of the most insidious threats to the Rule of Law is corruption, which can manifest at various levels and in different forms within the legal system.

Petty Corruption often involves small-scale bribes or favors exchanged to expedite bureaucratic processes, influence minor decisions, or avoid penalties. While seemingly insignificant, these acts of petty corruption can have a cumulative effect, eroding public trust in the legal system and creating a culture of impunity. For instance, a police officer accepting money to overlook a traffic violation, or a clerk demanding a bribe to process a document, are examples of petty corruption that can undermine the integrity of the legal system.

Grand Corruption, on the other hand, involves large-scale bribery and embezzlement by high-ranking officials, often influencing major legal outcomes or government contracts. This type of corruption can have devastating consequences, diverting public resources, distorting economic development, and undermining democratic institutions. Examples include government officials accepting bribes to award lucrative contracts to unqualified companies, or judges being bribed to rule in favor of powerful individuals or corporations.

Even more pernicious is **Systemic Corruption**, where corruption is deeply embedded in the institutions of the legal system, making it extremely difficult to address. This occurs when corruption becomes normalized and institutionalized, with corrupt practices being perpetuated by a network of individuals and organizations. Systemic corruption can manifest in the form of biased judicial appointments, corrupt law enforcement agencies, and a lack of effective oversight mechanisms.

The root causes of corruption are multifaceted. **Low salaries for legal professionals** can create an incentive for corruption, as individuals may be tempted to supplement their income through illicit means. A **lack of transparency** in legal processes makes it easier for corrupt practices to go undetected. **Weak oversight mechanisms** fail to hold corrupt officials accountable for their actions. And a **culture of impunity**, where powerful individuals are not held responsible for their wrongdoing, can further exacerbate the problem.

The consequences of corruption are far-reaching and devastating. Corruption distorts justice by allowing the wealthy and powerful to escape accountability, while the poor and vulnerable are disproportionately affected. It undermines economic development by creating an uneven playing field, discouraging investment, and diverting resources from essential public services. And it fuels social inequality by perpetuating cycles of poverty and marginalization. For example, a corrupt judge who accepts a bribe to rule against a poor litigant in a land dispute can effectively condemn that individual to a life of poverty and displacement.

Inequality Before the Law is another significant threat to the Rule of Law. It manifests in various forms, including economic, social, and geographic inequality.

Economic Inequality means that the wealthy can afford better legal representation, influencing legal outcomes in their favor. The high cost of lawyers, court fees, and other legal expenses can effectively bar the poor from accessing justice. Individuals with limited financial resources may be forced to represent themselves in court, or rely on overburdened and under-resourced public defenders, placing them at a significant disadvantage.

Social Inequality reflects discrimination based on race, ethnicity, gender, religion, or other factors. Systemic biases within the justice system can lead to discriminatory outcomes, with certain groups being disproportionately targeted by law enforcement, subjected to harsher penalties, and denied equal access to legal protections. For example, studies have shown that racial minorities are more likely to be stopped, searched, and arrested by police, and are more likely to receive longer prison sentences than their white counterparts for similar crimes. Implicit bias, also known as unconscious bias, plays a significant role.

Geographic Inequality arises when rural or marginalized communities lack access to legal services and adequate judicial infrastructure. Individuals living in remote areas may have to travel long distances to access a courthouse or a lawyer, and may face language barriers or other obstacles that hinder their ability to navigate the legal system. The inequality is apparent when comparing large urban areas to rural communities when accessing various judicial resources.

Inequality before the law perpetuates cycles of poverty and marginalization by denying individuals equal opportunities to participate in society, access education and employment, and protect their rights. It also undermines the legitimacy of the legal system, as people lose faith in its fairness and impartiality. The consequences of these forms of systemic inequalities is that those without resources simply cannot find justice, regardless of the validity of their claim.

Weak Enforcement of Laws further erodes the Rule of Law. This can stem from several factors, including political interference, corruption, and cultural norms.

Political Interference occurs when politicians protect individuals or groups from prosecution, undermining the independence of the judiciary and law enforcement agencies. When powerful individuals are able to manipulate the legal system for their own benefit, it sends a message that the law is not applied equally to all.

Corruption within law enforcement agencies, such as officers accepting bribes or turning a blind eye to criminal activity, further weakens the enforcement of laws. When law enforcement officials are corrupt, they are less likely to investigate and prosecute crimes effectively, creating a climate of impunity.

Cultural Norms that tolerate or even condone corruption and abuse of power can also contribute to weak enforcement of laws. In some societies, it may be considered acceptable for powerful individuals to use their influence to evade accountability, or for officials to demand bribes in exchange for services.

Weak enforcement undermines the deterrent effect of laws, as people realize that they can break the law without fear of punishment. This encourages further wrongdoing and erodes public trust in the government and the legal system. Citizens will be less likely to obey laws that are not consistently and fairly enforced, leading to a breakdown of social order.

In summary, the erosion of the Rule of Law is a complex and multifaceted problem, with far-reaching consequences for individuals, communities, and societies. Corruption, inequality, and weak enforcement of laws all contribute to the undermining of justice, eroding public trust, distorting economic development, and fueling social inequality. The consequences of this erosion are dire, leading to instability, conflict, and a breakdown of social order.

It is imperative that individuals, governments, and international organizations take concrete steps to protect and strengthen the Rule of Law. This requires a multi-pronged approach that addresses the root causes of corruption, promotes equality before the law, and strengthens law enforcement and judicial institutions. Low salaries must be increased, particularly in developing countries where the cost of living is incredibly high. Stricter enforcement is needed from the top down, to make sure laws are not only carried out, but also not being abused.

Individuals can play a role by demanding transparency and accountability from their leaders, reporting corruption, and advocating for legal reforms. Governments must strengthen oversight mechanisms, promote judicial independence, and ensure that law enforcement agencies are adequately resourced and trained. International organizations can provide technical assistance, financial support, and policy guidance to help countries strengthen their legal systems and combat corruption.

The Rule of Law is not just a legal concept; it is a fundamental pillar of a just, stable, and prosperous society. It is essential for protecting individual liberties, promoting economic development, and ensuring that all individuals have the opportunity to reach their full potential. Without the Rule of Law, societies are vulnerable to tyranny, oppression, and chaos.

Ultimately, the future of society depends on our collective commitment to upholding the principles of justice and the Rule of Law. Let us strive to create a world where everyone is treated equally under the law, where corruption is eradicated, and where justice prevails. For justice is not merely a legal ideal; it is the very essence of a civilized society, and the foundation upon which a better future can be built.

Let's explore how authoritarian regimes politicize the judiciary, undermine due process, and erode the rule of law.

THE CRITICAL ASPECT OF HOW AUTHORITARIAN REGIMES MAINTAIN POWER.

Here's a breakdown of the key elements and their implications:

- **Authoritarian Regimes:** These are systems of government characterized by strong central power and limited political freedoms. Examples include dictatorships, one-party states, and repressive monarchies.

- **Politicize the Judiciary:** This refers to the process of subjecting the judicial system to political influence and control. This can involve:

- **Appointing loyalists:** Filling judicial positions with individuals who are beholden to the regime rather than qualified legal professionals.

o **Pressuring judges:** Coercing judges to rule in favor of the government, often through threats, bribes, or promises of advancement.

o **Creating special courts:** Establishing courts with politically aligned judges to handle sensitive cases and silence dissent.

o **Ignoring judicial decisions:** Disregarding court rulings that contradict the regime's agenda.

o **Undermine Due Process:** Due process is the legal requirement that the government must respect all legal rights owed to a person. Undermining due process involves:

o **Arbitrary arrests and detentions:** Imprisoning individuals without evidence or legal justification.

o **Unfair trials:** Conducting trials that are biased, lack transparency, and deny defendants the right to a fair defense.

o **Torture and ill-treatment:** Using inhumane methods to extract confessions or intimidate political opponents.

o **Denial of legal representation:** Preventing individuals from accessing qualified lawyers.

o **Erode the Rule of Law:** The rule of law is the principle that all individuals and institutions, including the government, are subject to and accountable under the law. Authoritarian regimes erode the rule of law by:

o **Creating and enforcing laws selectively:** Applying laws to silence critics while exempting loyalists.

- **Acting above the law:** Operating outside the bounds of legal constraints and accountability.

- **Failing to enforce laws against those favored by the regime:** Creating a system of impunity for those in power.

- **Weakening or dismantling legal institutions:** Undermining the independence and effectiveness of courts, law enforcement agencies, and regulatory bodies.

OVERALL IMPLICATIONS:

When authoritarian regimes politicize the judiciary, undermine due process, and erode the rule of law, the following consequences often result:

- **Suppression of dissent:** Fear of arbitrary arrest and persecution silences opposition voices.

- **Human rights abuses:** The lack of legal protections leads to widespread violations of civil and political rights.

- **Economic instability:** Corruption and lack of transparency discourage investment and hinder economic development.

- **Social unrest:** Injustice and inequality can fuel anger and resentment, leading to protests and violence.

- **Weakening of democratic institutions:** The destruction of the rule of law makes it difficult to transition to a more democratic system.

Let's analyze the consequences of corruption, impunity, and the lack of legal protection for vulnerable populations.

Corruption, impunity, and the absence of adequate legal safeguards for vulnerable populations represent a toxic trifecta, undermining the very foundations of just and equitable societies. These intertwined issues, often mutually reinforcing, unleash a cascade of negative consequences that permeate political, economic, and social spheres, leaving a trail of instability, inequality, and human suffering.

One of the most insidious consequences of corruption is the **distortion of governance and the erosion of public trust**. When public officials prioritize personal gain over the common good, the efficacy of government institutions is severely compromised. Bribery, embezzlement, and cronyism divert resources away from essential services such as healthcare, education, and infrastructure development. For example, in countries riddled with corruption, funds allocated for building hospitals may be siphoned off, resulting in substandard facilities lacking essential equipment and personnel. This directly impacts the health and well-being of citizens, particularly those from vulnerable communities who rely most heavily on these public services. Moreover, when citizens witness blatant corruption without accountability, their faith in the legitimacy of the government diminishes, leading to apathy, disillusionment, and even social unrest. The Arab Spring uprisings, for instance, were fueled, in part, by widespread anger over corruption and a perceived lack of government responsiveness to the needs of the people.

Impunity, the exemption from punishment for wrongdoing, further exacerbates the damage caused by corruption. When corrupt officials and powerful individuals operate with the knowledge that they are above the law, it creates a culture of lawlessness and emboldens further malfeasance. This is particularly devastating for vulnerable populations, who are often the most susceptible to exploitation and abuse. Consider the prevalence of land grabbing in many developing countries. Corrupt officials, often in collusion with wealthy landowners or corporations, may illegally seize land belonging to indigenous communities or small farmers, displacing them from their homes and livelihoods. If these victims have no recourse to justice because the perpetrators are shielded by impunity, they are left with little hope of redress, perpetuating a cycle of poverty and marginalization. The lack of accountability also sends a dangerous message that crime pays, undermining the deterrent effect of the law and encouraging others to engage in corrupt practices.

The **absence of adequate legal protection for vulnerable populations** compounds the problems of corruption and impunity. Vulnerable groups, including women, children, minorities, refugees, and people with disabilities, often face systemic discrimination and marginalization that limits their access to justice. Discriminatory laws, biased judicial systems, and a lack of legal awareness can prevent them from asserting their rights and seeking redress for grievances. For example, in many countries, women face significant legal barriers to owning property, accessing credit, or inheriting assets. This economic disempowerment makes them more vulnerable to exploitation and abuse, and less able to protect themselves from the adverse effects of corruption and impunity. Similarly, refugees and migrants often lack legal status and are therefore at risk of being exploited by unscrupulous employers or subjected to human trafficking, with little or no access to legal remedies.

Furthermore, corruption and impunity often **undermine economic development and discourage foreign investment.** Investors are wary of doing business in countries where corruption is rampant, as it creates uncertainty, increases transaction costs, and exposes them to the risk of extortion and bribery. This leads to a decline in economic growth, job creation, and overall prosperity, further exacerbating inequality and poverty. The lack of legal protection for property rights, a direct consequence of corruption and weak governance, also discourages entrepreneurship and innovation, hindering long-term economic development.

Addressing the consequences of corruption, impunity, and the lack of legal protection for vulnerable populations requires a multifaceted approach. **Strengthening governance institutions, promoting transparency and accountability, and ensuring equal access to justice are essential steps.** This includes enacting and enforcing anti-corruption laws, establishing independent oversight bodies, protecting whistleblowers, and promoting media freedom. It also requires investing in legal aid programs, raising legal awareness among vulnerable populations, and reforming judicial systems to eliminate bias and discrimination. International cooperation is also crucial, particularly in combating transnational corruption and ensuring that perpetrators are held accountable for their actions.

The consequences of corruption, impunity, and the lack of legal protections for vulnerable populations are far-reaching and devastating. They erode public trust, undermine economic development, exacerbate inequality, and perpetuate human suffering. By addressing these intertwined issues through comprehensive reforms and a commitment to justice and the rule of law, societies can create a more equitable and sustainable future for all. Only through concerted efforts to combat corruption, ensure accountability, and protect the rights of vulnerable populations can we hope to build societies where justice prevails and everyone has the opportunity to thrive.

CASE STUDIES:

Politicized courts in Venezuela, Arbitrary detention in Egypt

Let's break down the concerns around politicized courts and arbitrary detention in each country, exploring their implications and potential consequences.

VENEZUELA: POLITICIZED COURTS AND EROSION OF THE RULE OF LAW

- **The Problem:** The Venezuelan judiciary, particularly the Supreme Tribunal of Justice (TSJ), has been accused of being heavily influenced by the ruling socialist party (PSUV). This politicization manifests in several ways:

- **Appointments and Removals:** Judges, especially at the TSJ level, are often appointed based on their loyalty to the government rather than their legal expertise or impartiality. There have been instances of judges being removed or pressured to resign if their rulings don't align with the government's interests.

- **Overruling the National Assembly:** The TSJ has repeatedly overruled decisions made by the National Assembly (the legislative branch), particularly when the Assembly was controlled by the opposition. This effectively neuters the legislative branch and concentrates power in the executive.

- **Legal Interpretations Favoring the Government:** The TSJ's legal interpretations often favor the government, even in cases where the law seems to dictate otherwise. This undermines the predictability and fairness of the legal system.

- o **Lack of Independence:** Judges often fear reprisals if they rule against the government, leading to self-censorship and biased rulings.

IMPACT:

- o **Undermining Democracy:** Weakening the separation of powers and allowing the executive branch to control the judiciary undermines the foundations of a democratic system.

- o **Impunity for Government Officials:** A politicized judiciary is less likely to hold government officials accountable for corruption, human rights abuses, or other wrongdoings.

- o **Erosion of Public Trust:** When people lose faith in the fairness and impartiality of the courts, they are less likely to respect the law or seek justice through legal channels.

- o **Suppression of Dissent:** The judiciary can be used to silence political opponents, activists, and journalists by bringing politically motivated charges against them.

- o **Economic Instability:** A lack of rule of law discourages foreign investment and hinders economic development. Businesses are less likely to invest in a country where contracts are not reliably enforced.

VENEZUELA:
ARBITRARY DETENTION

- o **The Problem:** Arbitrary detention, or imprisonment without due process, has been a persistent issue in Venezuela, particularly targeting political opponents, journalists, and activists.

o **Politically Motivated Arrests:** Individuals are often arrested on fabricated or flimsy charges, with the goal of silencing dissent or intimidating opposition groups.

o **Lack of Due Process:** Detainees are often denied access to lawyers, held incommunicado, and subjected to prolonged pre-trial detention.

o **Military Courts:** Civilians are sometimes tried in military courts, which lack the impartiality and procedural safeguards of civilian courts.

o **Harsh Prison Conditions:** Prisons in Venezuela are often overcrowded, unsanitary, and violent, and detainees may be subjected to torture or ill-treatment.

IMPACT:

o **Violation of Human Rights:** Arbitrary detention violates fundamental human rights, including the right to liberty, the right to a fair trial, and the right to be free from torture and ill-treatment.

o **Climate of Fear:** Arbitrary detention creates a climate of fear and repression, discouraging people from expressing their opinions or participating in political activities.

o **Weakening of Civil Society:** By targeting activists and journalists, arbitrary detention weakens civil society and makes it more difficult to hold the government accountable.

o **International Condemnation:** Arbitrary detention has been widely condemned by international human rights organizations and foreign governments.

EGYPT:
POLITICIZED COURTS AND EROSION OF THE RULE OF LAW

- o **The Problem:** Similar to Venezuela, concerns exist about the independence of the Egyptian judiciary, particularly after the 2013 coup led by then-General Abdel Fattah el-Sisi.

- o **Executive Influence:** The executive branch exerts significant influence over the judiciary through appointments, promotions, and disciplinary measures.

- o **Amendments Weakening Judicial Independence:** Constitutional amendments have expanded the president's power over judicial appointments and weakened the oversight role of judicial bodies.

- o **Mass Trials and Expedited Procedures:** Mass trials, often lacking due process, have become common, particularly in cases involving political opponents and alleged supporters of the Muslim Brotherhood. Expedited procedures limit the ability of defendants to present a defense.

- o **Military Courts:** A significant expansion of the jurisdiction of military courts to include civilians has occurred, particularly in cases involving national security or terrorism. Military courts lack the transparency and due process safeguards of civilian courts.

IMPACT:

- o **Suppression of Dissent:** The judiciary is used to silence political opponents, human rights activists, and journalists through politically motivated charges and unfair trials.

- **Impunity for Security Forces:** Allegations of human rights abuses by security forces are rarely investigated or prosecuted effectively, leading to impunity.

- **Erosion of Investor Confidence:** A lack of judicial independence and the rule of law deters foreign investment and economic development.

- **Fueling Radicalization:** Perceived injustices and lack of legal recourse can contribute to radicalization and violence.

- **Undermining the Legitimacy of the State:** When the legal system is seen as unfair and biased, it undermines the legitimacy of the state and its institutions.

EGYPT:
ARBITRARY DETENTION

- **The Problem:** Arbitrary detention is a widespread and systemic problem in Egypt.

- **Prolonged Pre-Trial Detention:** Individuals, particularly political opponents, are often held in pre-trial detention for months or even years without being formally charged or brought to trial.

- **"Revolving Door" Detentions:** When initial detention orders expire, individuals are often re-arrested on new charges to prolong their imprisonment.

- **Enforced Disappearances:** There have been credible reports of enforced disappearances, where individuals are abducted by security forces and their whereabouts are unknown.

- o **Poor Prison Conditions:** Prisons in Egypt are often overcrowded, unsanitary, and lack adequate medical care. Detainees are often subjected to torture, ill-treatment, and denial of family visits.

- o **Targeting of Human Rights Defenders:** Human rights defenders, lawyers, and journalists who document and report on human rights abuses are often targeted with arbitrary arrest and detention.

IMPACT:

- o **Human Rights Violations:** Arbitrary detention violates a range of human rights, including the right to liberty, the right to a fair trial, and the right to be free from torture and ill-treatment.

- o **Climate of Fear:** Arbitrary detention creates a climate of fear and discourages dissent and political participation.

- o **Weakening of Civil Society:** The targeting of human rights defenders and civil society organizations weakens their ability to monitor and report on human rights abuses.

- o **Damage to Egypt's International Reputation:** Arbitrary detention has led to widespread international condemnation and has damaged Egypt's reputation as a reliable partner.

- o **Radicalization:** Experiences of arbitrary detention and ill-treatment can contribute to radicalization and violence.

COMMON THEMES AND POTENTIAL SOLUTIONS

Several common themes emerge from the situations in Venezuela and Egypt:

- **Executive Overreach:** In both countries, the executive branch has systematically undermined the independence of the judiciary and expanded its own powers at the expense of other branches of government.

- **Suppression of Dissent:** The legal system is used as a tool to silence political opponents, activists, and journalists.

- **Lack of Accountability:** Government officials and security forces are rarely held accountable for human rights abuses.

- **Erosion of Public Trust:** The public's faith in the fairness and impartiality of the legal system has been eroded.

- **Potential Solutions:** Addressing these complex challenges requires a multifaceted approach that includes:

- **Strengthening Judicial Independence:** Implementing constitutional and legal reforms to guarantee the independence of the judiciary, including transparent and merit-based appointment processes, security of tenure for judges, and protection from political interference.

- **Reforming Criminal Justice Systems:** Amending laws to ensure due process rights, limit pre-trial detention, and end the practice of trying civilians in military courts.

- **Promoting Accountability**: Establishing independent mechanisms to investigate and prosecute allegations of human rights abuses by government officials and security forces.

- **Protecting Civil Society:** Enacting laws and policies that protect the rights of human rights defenders, journalists, and civil society organizations to operate freely.

- **International Pressure:** International organizations, foreign governments, and human rights groups can play a role by:

- **Monitoring and Reporting:** Documenting and publicly reporting on human rights abuses and violations of the rule of law.

- **Sanctions**: Imposing targeted sanctions on individuals and entities responsible for human rights abuses and corruption.

- **Conditioning Aid:** Conditioning economic and military aid on improvements in human rights and the rule of law.

- **Providing Assistance:** Supporting civil society organizations, human rights defenders, and independent media.

- **Promoting Education and Awareness:** Educating the public about human rights and the rule of law.

It's crucial to recognize that these are long-term challenges that require sustained effort and commitment from both domestic and international actors. While the situations in Venezuela and Egypt are distinct, the underlying principles of the rule of law and respect for human rights are universal and must be upheld.

THE FORGOTTEN REFUGEES
The Human Cost of Conflict and Persecution

Let's analyze the global refugee crisis and the challenges of protecting vulnerable populations.

The 21st century is marked by unprecedented levels of displacement, creating a global refugee crisis that demands urgent attention. While headlines often focus on geopolitical strategies and economic implications, it is crucial to remember the human cost of conflict and persecution – the stories of millions forced to flee their homes, their lives shattered, and their futures uncertain. This essay examines the multifaceted dimensions of the global refugee crisis, highlighting the challenges of protecting vulnerable populations and underscoring the urgent need for comprehensive and compassionate solutions.

The term "refugee," as defined by the 1951 Refugee Convention, encompasses individuals who have fled their country of origin due to a well-founded fear of being persecuted for reasons of race, religion, nationality, membership of a particular social group, or political opinion. However, the reality of displacement is far more complex than this definition suggests. Beyond those formally recognized as refugees, there are internally displaced persons (IDPs) who have fled their homes but remain within their country's borders, asylum seekers awaiting the outcome of their refugee status claims, and stateless individuals lacking any recognized nationality. These populations, often overlooked and underserved, constitute a significant portion of those forcibly displaced.

Conflict remains a primary driver of displacement. Protracted wars, civil unrest, and the rise of violent extremism in regions like Syria,

Yemen, Afghanistan, and the Democratic Republic of Congo have forced millions to seek refuge in neighboring countries or further afield. The Syrian civil war, for example, has created the largest refugee crisis in modern history, with millions displaced internally and externally, straining the resources of host countries like Lebanon, Jordan, and Turkey. These countries, often facing their own economic and political challenges, struggle to provide adequate shelter, food, healthcare, and education to the influx of refugees.

Beyond conflict, persecution based on identity, beliefs, or political affiliations also contributes significantly to displacement. Ethnic cleansing, religious discrimination, and the suppression of political dissent force individuals and communities to flee in search of safety. The Rohingya crisis in Myanmar, where a Muslim minority group has faced systematic persecution and violence, resulting in a mass exodus to Bangladesh, exemplifies this tragic reality. Similarly, LGBTQ+ individuals in countries where homosexuality is criminalized or faces severe social stigma are often forced to seek asylum elsewhere.

The challenges of protecting vulnerable refugee populations are immense. The journey to safety is often perilous, with refugees facing risks of exploitation, trafficking, and violence. Women and children are particularly vulnerable, often becoming victims of sexual assault, forced labor, and recruitment into armed groups. Refugee camps, while providing a temporary refuge, can become overcrowded and unsanitary, leading to the spread of disease and exacerbating existing vulnerabilities. Access to education, healthcare, and livelihood opportunities is often limited, hindering refugees' ability to rebuild their lives and integrate into host communities.

The rise of xenophobia and anti-immigrant sentiment in many countries poses a significant threat to the protection of refugees. Political narratives that demonize refugees as a burden on society or a threat to national security fuel discrimination, restrict access to asylum, and undermine efforts to integrate refugees into host communities. The implementation of restrictive border policies, such as those witnessed in Europe and the United States, further complicates the situation, leaving many refugees stranded in precarious situations or forced to take dangerous routes in search of safety.

Addressing the global refugee crisis requires a multifaceted approach that encompasses both immediate humanitarian assistance and long-term solutions. Increased funding for humanitarian organizations like UNHCR and the World Food Programme is essential to provide life-saving assistance to refugees and IDPs. Strengthening international cooperation and burden-sharing mechanisms is crucial to ensure that host countries are adequately supported in their efforts to accommodate refugees. Investing in education, job training, and integration programs can help refugees become self-sufficient and contribute to the economies of their host countries.

However, humanitarian assistance alone is not enough. Addressing the root causes of displacement – conflict, persecution, and inequality – is essential to prevent future refugee crises. This requires concerted efforts to promote peace and security, uphold human rights, and foster inclusive and sustainable development. Investing in conflict prevention and resolution, promoting good governance and the rule of law, and addressing the underlying drivers of inequality and discrimination are crucial steps in creating a world where people are not forced to flee their homes in search of safety.

In conclusion, the global refugee crisis is a complex and multifaceted challenge that demands a comprehensive and compassionate response. Protecting vulnerable refugee populations requires not only providing immediate humanitarian assistance but also addressing the root causes of displacement and fostering a global environment of tolerance, respect, and solidarity. By recognizing the human cost of conflict and persecution and upholding the principles of international law and human rights, we can work towards a future where all individuals have the right to live in safety and dignity, free from fear and persecution. The forgotten refugees deserve to be remembered, their stories heard, and their rights protected. Only then can we hope to build a more just and equitable world for all.

Let's analyze the role of conflict, persecution, and climate change in driving displacement.

THE INTERTWINED DRIVERS OF DISPLACEMENT

Displacement, the forced movement of people from their homes and communities, is a complex global challenge with far-reaching consequences. While the reasons behind displacement are multifaceted and often interconnected, three primary drivers stand out: conflict, persecution, and climate change. Each of these factors can independently force individuals and communities to seek refuge elsewhere, but increasingly, they interact and exacerbate one another, creating a perfect storm of displacement pressures. Understanding the specific roles of these drivers, as well as their intricate relationships, is crucial for developing effective strategies to address and mitigate the global displacement crisis.

CONFLICT AS A CATALYST FOR DISPLACEMENT

Armed conflict, both within and between states, has historically been a major driver of displacement. Violence, instability, and the breakdown of social order associated with conflict force people to flee their homes in search of safety. The devastating effects of war, including direct attacks on civilians, destruction of infrastructure, and widespread human rights abuses, create an environment where survival becomes impossible.

The Syrian Civil War, for example, has resulted in one of the largest displacement crises in recent history. Millions of Syrians have been internally displaced, while millions more have sought refuge in neighboring countries and beyond. The conflict, characterized by brutal violence, including the use of chemical weapons and indiscriminate bombings, has rendered vast areas of the country uninhabitable. Similarly, ongoing conflicts in regions like Yemen, the Democratic Republic of Congo, and Myanmar continue to generate massive displacement flows.

Beyond direct violence, conflict also disrupts essential services, such as healthcare, education, and access to food and water. This breakdown of societal structures further compels people to leave in search of basic necessities and a semblance of normalcy. The threat of recruitment into armed groups, particularly for young people, is another significant factor driving displacement in conflict zones. Addressing conflict-induced displacement requires not only humanitarian assistance but also sustained efforts to resolve underlying political grievances, promote peacebuilding, and ensure accountability for war crimes.

PERSECUTION: A TARGETED THREAT

Persecution, defined as the systematic ill-treatment of an individual or group by another group, is another powerful driver of displacement. This persecution can be based on a variety of factors, including race, religion, ethnicity, political opinion, or membership in a particular social group. When persecution becomes severe and poses an imminent threat to life and liberty, individuals and communities are often left with no choice but to flee.

The Rohingya crisis in Myanmar is a stark example of persecution-driven displacement. The Rohingya, a Muslim minority group, have faced decades of discrimination and violence at the hands of the Myanmar government and military. In 2017, a brutal military crackdown forced hundreds of thousands of Rohingya to flee to neighboring Bangladesh, creating a massive refugee crisis. The persecution included mass killings, sexual violence, and the systematic destruction of Rohingya villages.

Religious persecution is a recurring theme in displacement crises around the world. Christians, Muslims, and other religious minorities often face discrimination and violence in countries where religious freedom is not protected. Political persecution, targeting dissidents, journalists, and human rights activists, also forces many to seek asylum in other countries. Addressing persecution-driven displacement requires strong international mechanisms to protect human rights, hold perpetrators accountable, and promote tolerance and inclusion. Furthermore, addressing misinformation and hate speech that fuels persecution is also a critical step.

CLIMATE CHANGE: A GROWING FORCE MULTIPLIER

Climate change is increasingly recognized as a significant driver of displacement, although its impact is often indirect and intertwined with other factors. Climate-related disasters, such as floods, droughts, and extreme weather events, can destroy homes, livelihoods, and infrastructure, forcing people to move in search of safety and resources. Sea-level rise threatens coastal communities, while desertification and land degradation can render agricultural lands unproductive, leading to displacement and migration.

The impact of climate change on displacement is particularly acute in vulnerable regions that are already facing conflict, poverty, and political instability. For example, in the Sahel region of Africa, climate change is exacerbating existing resource scarcity and contributing to conflicts between farmers and herders, leading to displacement. Similarly, in Bangladesh, rising sea levels and increased flooding are displacing millions of people, many of whom are migrating to urban areas or seeking refuge in other countries.

While climate change can directly cause displacement through sudden-onset disasters, it also acts as a "threat multiplier," exacerbating existing vulnerabilities and increasing the risk of conflict and persecution. For instance, climate-induced resource scarcity can fuel competition over land and water, leading to social tensions and violence. Addressing climate-related displacement requires a multi-pronged approach that includes mitigating climate change, adapting to its impacts, and providing assistance to those who are displaced. This also calls for recognizing "climate refugees" under international law, which is currently a contentious issue.

THE INTERCONNECTEDNESS OF DISPLACEMENT DRIVERS

It is important to recognize that conflict, persecution, and climate change are often interconnected and mutually reinforcing. Climate change can exacerbate resource scarcity and competition, leading to conflict and displacement. Conflict can weaken governance structures and create opportunities for persecution. Persecution can drive people to migrate to regions that are vulnerable to climate change, increasing their exposure to environmental risks.

For example, the conflict in Darfur, Sudan, was fueled in part by competition over dwindling resources due to climate change. The conflict, in turn, led to widespread displacement and human rights abuses. Similarly, in Somalia, drought and famine have exacerbated existing political instability and conflict, leading to further displacement.

Understanding the complex interplay between these drivers is crucial for developing effective and sustainable solutions to the displacement crisis. A holistic approach is needed that addresses the root causes of conflict, protects human rights, mitigates climate change, and provides assistance to those who are displaced.

Conflict, persecution, and climate change are powerful drivers of displacement, each with its own distinct characteristics and consequences. While these factors can operate independently, they are increasingly intertwined and mutually reinforcing, creating complex and challenging displacement scenarios. Addressing the global displacement crisis requires a comprehensive and coordinated approach that tackles the root causes of these drivers, protects the rights of displaced people, and promotes sustainable solutions to displacement. This includes conflict resolution, human rights protection, climate change mitigation and adaptation, and humanitarian assistance. Only through such a multifaceted approach can we hope to alleviate the suffering of those who are forced to flee their homes and build a more just and sustainable world for all.

Let's discuss the moral and legal obligations of states to provide refuge and assistance to refugees.

The plight of refugees, individuals forced to flee their homelands due to persecution, war, or violence, presents a profound challenge to the international community. While often framed as a matter of political expediency or national security, the question of how states should respond to refugees rests upon a bedrock of both moral and legal obligations. Examining these obligations reveals a compelling argument for providing refuge and assistance, grounded in fundamental principles of human dignity, international law, and shared responsibility.

The moral obligation to aid refugees stems from the inherent worth and dignity of every human being. Kant's categorical imperative, which emphasizes treating individuals as ends in themselves rather than merely as means, provides a strong philosophical foundation. To turn away a refugee in dire need, especially when their life is at risk, is to disregard their fundamental humanity and deny them their basic right to survival. This moral imperative is further strengthened by the principle of beneficence, which suggests that those with the capacity to help should alleviate suffering whenever possible. Wealthy and stable states, possessing the resources and infrastructure to support refugees, arguably have a heightened moral duty to do so. Furthermore, notions of global justice demand a more equitable distribution of responsibility. If certain states, through their actions or inaction, contribute to the conditions that create refugees (whether through conflict, economic policies, or environmental damage), they bear a particular moral responsibility to assist those displaced. The concept of "common but differentiated responsibilities," often invoked in climate change discussions, also applies here, acknowledging that while all states have a responsibility, those with greater capacity should shoulder a larger burden.

The legal obligations of states towards refugees are primarily enshrined in international law, most notably in the 1951 Refugee Convention and its 1967 Protocol. This foundational document defines a refugee as someone with a well-founded fear of being persecuted for reasons of race, religion, nationality, membership of a particular social group, or political opinion, who is outside the country of their nationality and is unable or, owing to such fear, is unwilling to avail themself of the protection of that country. The core principle of the Refugee Convention is *non-refoulement*, which prohibits states from returning refugees to territories where their lives or freedoms would be threatened. This principle, widely considered a cornerstone of international refugee law, creates a binding legal obligation on signatory states to refrain from actions that would endanger refugees.

Beyond *non-refoulement*, the Refugee Convention outlines a range of rights and obligations related to the treatment of refugees. These include the right to access courts, education, and employment, as well as the right to freedom of movement within the host country. While the Convention does not explicitly mandate states to provide asylum to all refugees, it does create a framework for international cooperation and burden-sharing. The principle of international cooperation, as enshrined in the UN Charter, implies that states should work together to address global challenges like refugee crises. This cooperation can take various forms, including providing financial assistance to host countries, resettling refugees, and addressing the root causes of displacement. Regional agreements, such as the European Union's asylum system, further elaborate on these obligations and aim to harmonize asylum procedures and ensure a more equitable distribution of asylum seekers among member states.

However, the interpretation and implementation of these legal obligations are often contested. States frequently invoke arguments of national security, economic constraints, and cultural preservation to justify restrictive asylum policies. The rise of anti-immigrant sentiment in many countries has further fueled the debate, leading to increasingly stringent border controls, detention of asylum seekers, and limitations on access to asylum procedures. Some states argue that the Refugee Convention places an undue burden on them, especially when faced with large-scale refugee influxes. They contend that the principle of *non-refoulement* should be interpreted narrowly and that they have the right to prioritize the interests of their own citizens. The concept of "safe country of origin" is often invoked to justify the return of asylum seekers to countries deemed to be generally safe, even if individual circumstances may warrant protection.

These arguments, while understandable in the context of national interests, must be carefully scrutinized. The principle of *non-refoulement* is a fundamental safeguard against persecution and should not be easily disregarded. States have a responsibility to ensure that asylum procedures are fair and efficient, and that asylum seekers have access to legal representation and due process. While national security concerns are legitimate, they should not be used as a pretext to deny asylum to those who genuinely fear persecution. Furthermore, economic constraints should not be used to justify inhumane treatment of refugees. International cooperation and burden-sharing are essential to ensure that host countries receive the necessary support to manage refugee populations.

In conclusion, both moral and legal obligations compel states to provide refuge and assistance to refugees. The inherent dignity of every human being demands that we alleviate suffering and protect those who are most vulnerable. International law, as embodied in the Refugee Convention and related instruments, provides a framework for ensuring the protection of refugees' rights and promoting international cooperation. While challenges and complexities undoubtedly exist, states must uphold their moral and legal responsibilities to refugees, recognizing that a humane and just response to displacement is not only a matter of legal compliance but also a reflection of our shared humanity. Ignoring these obligations erodes the very foundations of international law and undermines the principles of justice and compassion that should guide our actions. The question is not whether states *should* help refugees, but *how* they can best fulfill their responsibilities in a manner that is both effective and humane.

REBUILDING TRUST
Strengthening Institutions and Promoting
Civic Engagement

Let's examine strategies for strengthening democratic institutions, promoting civic engagement, and restoring trust in government.

STRENGTHENING DEMOCRATIC INSTITUTIONS:

- **SPECIFICITY:** This initiative focuses on strengthening key democratic institutions including:

- **THE JUDICIARY (COURTS):** Ensuring equal access to justice and upholding the rule of law.

- **ELECTORAL SYSTEMS:** Guaranteeing free, fair, and secure elections that reflect the will of the people.

- **LEGISLATIVE BODIES (PARLIAMENTS/CONGRESSES):** Improving lawmaking processes and effective oversight of the executive branch.

- **INDEPENDENT REGULATORY AGENCIES:** Protecting the public interest through impartial and evidence-based regulation.

- o **LAW ENFORCEMENT AGENCIES:** Ensuring fair and equal application of the law, and accountability of officers.

- o **MEDIA AND INFORMATION ECOSYSTEM:** Promoting accurate and diverse reporting, combatting misinformation, and ensuring freedom of the press.

- o **AREAS OF IMPROVEMENT:** These institutions will be strengthened by focusing on:

- o **TRANSPARENCY:** Making processes and information readily accessible to the public.

- o **ACCOUNTABILITY:** Holding individuals and institutions responsible for their actions.

- o **RESPONSIVENESS:** Ensuring institutions are receptive to the needs and concerns of citizens.

- o **EFFICIENCY:** Streamlining processes and resource allocation to improve performance.

- o **INDEPENDENCE:** Protecting institutions from undue political influence.

- o **RULE OF LAW:** Ensuring consistent and impartial application of laws.

EXAMPLES OF STRATEGIES:

REFORMING CAMPAIGN finance laws to reduce the influence of special interests and ensure equitable access to political participation.

IMPROVING ACCESS TO VOTING and modernizing election administration through measures like online registration, automatic voter registration, and expanded early voting options.

INCREASING TRANSPARENCY in government decision-making through open data initiatives, public consultations, and mandatory disclosure requirements.

ENHANCING JUDICIAL INDEPENDENCE through merit-based appointment processes and robust protections against political interference.

IMPLEMENTING WHISTLEBLOWER protection laws to encourage reporting of corruption and misconduct.

INVESTING in the training and resources needed by government staff to combat misinformation and disinformation.

ESTABLISHING INDEPENDENT OVERSIGHT mechanisms for law enforcement agencies to address public concerns about police brutality and promote accountability.

SMART Objectives:

- o INCREASE TRANSPARENCY SCORES

- o REDUCE THE TIME IT TAKES TO RESOLVE LEGAL CASES

- o INCREASE THE NUMBER OF WOMEN AND MINORITY APPOINTMENTS

PROMOTING CIVIC ENGAGEMENT:

TARGET AUDIENCES: This initiative targets all citizens, with specific emphasis on:

YOUNG PEOPLE: Encouraging participation in democratic processes from an early age.

MARGINALIZED COMMUNITIES: Addressing barriers to participation faced by historically excluded groups (e.g., racial minorities, low-income communities, people with disabilities).

NEW IMMIGRANTS: Providing resources and opportunities for civic integration.

METHODS OF ENGAGEMENT:

- **DEVELOPING EDUCATIONAL PROGRAMS** to increase civic literacy and knowledge of government processes in schools and communities.

- **SUPPORTING COMMUNITY-BASED ORGANIZATIONS** that facilitate dialogue, voter registration drives, and issue advocacy.

- **UTILIZING TECHNOLOGY** and social media platforms to disseminate information, facilitate online forums, and connect citizens with their elected officials.

- **CREATING OPPORTUNITIES** for citizens to participate in policy development and decision-making through town hall meetings, public hearings, and online consultation platforms.

o **PROMOTING PARTICIPATORY BUDGETING** processes where citizens directly allocate public funds for local projects.

o **ENCOURAGING VOLUNTEERISM** and service learning through national service programs and partnerships with non-profit organizations.

SMART Objectives:

INCREASE VOTER TURNOUT among youth (18-29) in the next general election.

INCREASE PARTICIPATION IN COMMUNITY FORUMS AND TOWN HALL MEETINGS by residents of marginalized communities.

EXPAND CIVIC EDUCATION PROGRAMS to reach an increased number of schools and community organizations within 4 years.

INCREASE THE NUMBER OF CITIZEN-INITIATED POLICY PROPOSALS submitted through online platforms.

RESTORING TRUST IN GOVERNMENT:
ADDRESSING ROOT CAUSES:

o Acknowledging the factors that contribute to distrust, including:

o Corruption and abuse of power.

o Lack of transparency and accountability.

o Perceived inequality and economic injustice.

- Political polarization and partisan gridlock.

- Misinformation and the erosion of trust in credible sources of information.

- Lack of government responsiveness to citizens' needs.

- Inefficient and bureaucratic processes.

STRATEGIES FOR RESTORATION:

- **ENACTING AND ENFORCING** anti-corruption laws, and strengthening ethics regulations for public officials.

- **PROMOTING TRANSPARENCY** and open government principles across all levels of government.

- **ADDRESSING ECONOMIC INEQUALITY** through policies that promote fair wages, access to education, and affordable healthcare.

- **ENCOURAGING CIVIL DISCOURSE** and compromise through initiatives to bridge political divides.

- **COMBATING MISINFORMATION** and disinformation through media literacy campaigns and partnerships with fact-checking organizations.

- **IMPROVING GOVERNMENT SERVICE** delivery and responsiveness to citizen concerns.

- **SIMPLIFYING GOVERNMENT PROCESSES** and reducing bureaucratic red tape.

MEASURABLE OUTCOMES:

- o **INCREASING PUBLIC CONFIDENCE** in government institutions (measured by public opinion surveys).

- o **IMPROVING CITIZEN SATISFACTION** with government services (measured by feedback mechanisms and customer satisfaction surveys).

- o **BOOSTING VOTER TURNOUT** in local, regional, and national elections.

- o **REDUCING POLITICAL POLARIZATION** (measured by surveys assessing political attitudes and partisan animosity and legislative productivity).

- o **ENHANCING THE CREDIBILITY OF GOVERNMENT INFORMATION** sources (measured by media trust surveys - this is more indirect but related to the public sphere of truth finding).

SMART Objectives:

- o Increase public confidence in government.

- o Improve citizen satisfaction with government services.

- o Reduce the percentage of citizens identifying as "strongly opposed" to the opposing political party.

- o Increase the number of bi-partisan bills passed by the legislature.

Let's address the importance of education, transparency, and accountability.

THE PILLARS OF PROGRESS
Education, Transparency, and Accountability in a Globalized World

In an increasingly interconnected and complex world, the pursuit of progress hinges on a trifecta of crucial elements: education, transparency, and accountability. These three pillars form the foundation upon which stable societies are built, economies flourish, and individual potential is realized. Their absence breeds corruption, inequality, and stagnation, while their robust presence fosters innovation, trust, and sustainable development. This essay will explore the significance of education, transparency, and accountability, highlighting examples of positive reforms and initiatives from around the globe that demonstrate their transformative power.

The Indispensable Role of Education

Education is more than the acquisition of knowledge; it is the engine of societal advancement. It empowers individuals with critical thinking skills, enabling them to analyze information, solve problems, and contribute meaningfully to their communities. A well-educated populace is more likely to participate in democratic processes, engage in informed decision-making, and contribute to economic growth. Furthermore, education fosters innovation, driving scientific discoveries, technological advancements, and creative expression.

The benefits of education extend far beyond the individual level. Nations with higher levels of education consistently demonstrate greater economic prosperity, improved health outcomes, and reduced crime rates. Education promotes social mobility, allowing individuals from disadvantaged backgrounds to climb the socioeconomic ladder and break cycles of poverty. It also cultivates tolerance and understanding, fostering empathy and respect for diverse cultures and perspectives.

Across the globe, numerous initiatives aim to improve access to quality education. In Finland, for example, the education system is renowned for its emphasis on equity, teacher training, and student-centered learning. There, teachers are highly respected professionals, and the curriculum focuses on developing well-rounded individuals rather than simply preparing students for standardized tests. This approach has consistently yielded impressive results, with Finnish students ranking among the highest in international assessments.

In developing countries, organizations like the Global Partnership for Education (GPE) are working to strengthen education systems and ensure that all children have the opportunity to learn. The GPE provides funding and technical assistance to partner countries, supporting initiatives such as teacher training, curriculum development, and the construction of schools. These efforts are crucial for breaking the cycle of poverty and empowering future generations. Moreover, the rise of online learning platforms, like Coursera and edX, are democratizing access to education, providing affordable and flexible learning opportunities to individuals around the world, regardless of their location or socioeconomic status. These platforms not only provide access to formal education but also vocational training, equipping individuals with skills needed to excel in the global job market.

TRANSPARENCY:
Shedding Light on Governance and Business

Transparency, the principle of openness and accessibility of information, is essential for fostering trust and accountability in both government and the private sector. When information is readily available to the public, citizens can hold their leaders accountable for their actions, and businesses can operate ethically and responsibly. Transparency reduces corruption, promotes efficiency, and strengthens democratic institutions.

In the realm of governance, transparency initiatives such as freedom of information laws empower citizens to access government documents and data, ensuring that decision-making processes are open to scrutiny. Open budget initiatives promote transparency in public finances, allowing citizens to track how taxpayer money is being spent. These measures help to prevent corruption, ensure that resources are used effectively, and build public trust in government.

Estonia provides a compelling example of the power of transparency in governance. The country has embraced e-governance, making a wide range of public services available online and providing citizens with access to government data. This has not only improved efficiency and reduced bureaucracy but has also increased transparency and accountability. Citizens can track the progress of government initiatives, monitor spending, and participate in online consultations, fostering a more participatory and responsive government.

Transparency is equally important in the private sector. Companies that operate transparently are more likely to attract investors, retain customers, and build a strong reputation. Initiatives such as corporate social responsibility (CSR) reporting require companies to disclose information about their environmental and social impact, allowing stakeholders to assess their performance and hold them accountable.

The Extractive Industries Transparency Initiative (EITI) promotes transparency in the oil, gas, and mining industries, ensuring that revenues from natural resources are used for the benefit of the population.

ACCOUNTABILITY:
Ensuring Responsibility and Consequences

Accountability is the principle that individuals and organizations are responsible for their actions and must be held accountable for their consequences. It is the mechanism by which transparency translates into meaningful change. Without accountability, transparency is merely a window dressing, providing information without any real power to influence behavior.

Accountability mechanisms can take many forms, including legal frameworks, regulatory bodies, and civil society organizations. Independent judiciaries and law enforcement agencies are essential for holding individuals accountable for criminal behavior. Regulatory bodies oversee industries and enforce standards of conduct, ensuring that businesses operate ethically and responsibly. Civil society organizations play a crucial role in monitoring government and corporate behavior, exposing corruption, and advocating for greater accountability.

The International Criminal Court (ICC) is an example of an international accountability mechanism. It investigates and prosecutes individuals accused of the most serious crimes of concern to the international community, such as genocide, war crimes, and crimes against humanity. While the ICC's effectiveness is debated, it represents an important step towards holding individuals accountable for atrocities that would otherwise go unpunished.

At the national level, independent anti-corruption agencies play a vital role in combating graft and promoting accountability. These agencies investigate allegations of corruption, prosecute offenders, and implement preventive measures. In some countries, such as Hong Kong, these agencies have been highly successful in reducing corruption and building public trust in government. Moreover, whistleblower protection laws are crucial components to fostering accountability. By protecting individuals who report wrongdoing, these laws encourage transparency and help uncover misconduct that might otherwise remain hidden.

Synergy and the Path Forward

Education, transparency, and accountability are not mutually exclusive; rather, they are interdependent and mutually reinforcing. Education empowers citizens to demand transparency and hold their leaders accountable. Transparency provides the information needed to assess performance and identify areas for improvement. Accountability ensures that individuals and organizations are held responsible for their actions, creating incentives for ethical behavior and good governance.

Moving forward, it is essential to strengthen these three pillars in all societies. This requires investing in education, promoting transparency in governance and business, and establishing robust accountability mechanisms. It also requires fostering a culture of integrity and ethical behavior, where individuals are encouraged to speak out against corruption and injustice.

The challenges are significant, but the potential rewards are even greater. By embracing education, transparency, and accountability, we can build more just, equitable, and prosperous societies for all. These are not merely abstract ideals; they are the essential ingredients for a brighter future. The examples from Finland, Estonia, and the work of organizations like GPE and EITI demonstrate that progress is possible when these principles are prioritized and implemented effectively. The journey may be long, but the destination is a world where opportunity is accessible to all, where power is held in check, and where the common good prevails.

COMBATING DISINFORMATION
Promoting Media Literacy and Critical Thinking

Let's address strategies for combating disinformation, promoting media literacy, and fostering critical thinking.

In an era defined by instant communication and a deluge of information, the weaponization of disinformation has emerged as a significant threat to democratic societies and individual well-being. The rapid spread of deliberately false or misleading information, often referred to as "fake news," undermines public trust, polarizes communities, and can even incite violence. Combating this insidious phenomenon requires a multifaceted approach centered on promoting media literacy, fostering critical thinking skills, and leveraging technology and regulation responsibly.

One of the most effective long-term strategies for countering disinformation is to empower individuals with the tools to discern truth from falsehood. This is where media literacy and critical thinking become paramount. Media literacy, in its broadest sense, encompasses the ability to access, analyze, evaluate, and create media in various forms. It equips individuals to understand how media messages are constructed, what biases they might contain, and what underlying agendas they may serve. Critical thinking, meanwhile, builds upon media literacy by encouraging rigorous inquiry, logical reasoning, and objective evaluation of evidence. It involves questioning assumptions, identifying logical fallacies, and forming independent judgments based on credible information.

The cornerstone of promoting media literacy and critical thinking lies within the education system. Integrating media literacy into school curricula, from primary to higher education, is crucial. Students should be taught how to identify different types of media bias, assess the credibility of sources, and recognize common disinformation tactics, such as manipulated images and emotionally charged headlines. Beyond formal education, public awareness campaigns, workshops, and online resources can play a vital role in reaching wider audiences, including adults who may not have had the opportunity to develop these skills. These initiatives should focus on practical techniques, such as reverse image searching, fact-checking websites, and cross-referencing information from multiple sources.

Technology, while often implicated in the spread of disinformation, can also be a powerful tool in its mitigation. Artificial intelligence (AI) and machine learning algorithms are being developed to detect and flag potentially misleading content. These technologies can analyze text, images, and video for inconsistencies, anomalies, and patterns associated with disinformation campaigns. Social media platforms, in particular, have a responsibility to invest in these technologies and implement proactive measures to identify and remove fake accounts, bots, and coordinated disinformation networks. Furthermore, platforms should provide clear and transparent labelling for potentially misleading content, allowing users to make informed decisions about what they choose to believe and share.

However, relying solely on technological solutions is insufficient. Algorithmic detection can be fallible, and sophisticated disinformation actors are constantly evolving their tactics to evade detection. Human oversight and fact-checking remain essential. Independent fact-checking organizations play a crucial role in verifying claims made in the news and online, providing accurate and unbiased information to the public. These organizations often adhere to strict journalistic standards and operate with transparency, allowing users to assess their credibility. Furthermore, collaborative fact-checking initiatives, involving citizen journalists and subject matter experts, can help to scale up efforts and address the vast volume of disinformation circulating online.

The role of regulation in fighting fake news is a complex and often contentious issue. While censorship is incompatible with democratic values and freedom of expression, some level of regulation may be necessary to address the most egregious forms of disinformation, particularly those that incite violence, promote hate speech, or interfere with democratic processes. However, any regulatory framework must be carefully designed to avoid stifling legitimate speech and must be subject to rigorous oversight to prevent abuse. Potential regulatory measures could include holding social media platforms accountable for the content hosted on their platforms, requiring transparency in online advertising, and implementing stricter penalties for malicious actors engaging in disinformation campaigns.

Examples of successful media literacy programs and fact-checking initiatives offer valuable insights into effective strategies for combating disinformation. Finland, for example, has implemented a comprehensive media literacy curriculum in its schools, starting at a very young age. This sustained focus on media literacy has been credited with making Finnish citizens more resilient to disinformation and more likely to critically evaluate information sources. In the United States, organizations like Snopes and PolitiFact have established a strong track record of fact-checking political claims and debunking misleading information online. Their rigorous methodology and commitment to accuracy have earned them a reputation as trusted sources of information.

Furthermore, collaborative initiatives, such as the First Draft Coalition, bring together journalists, technologists, and researchers to develop and share best practices for combating disinformation. These collaborations are essential for fostering innovation and ensuring that efforts to combat disinformation are coordinated and effective.

In conclusion, combating disinformation requires a comprehensive and collaborative approach that encompasses education, technology, and regulation. By empowering individuals with media literacy and critical thinking skills, leveraging technology to detect and flag misleading content, and implementing responsible regulatory measures, we can foster a more informed and resilient society that is better equipped to navigate the complex information landscape and resist the harmful effects of disinformation. The fight against fake news is not just a technological or regulatory challenge; it is a societal imperative that requires the active participation of individuals, institutions, and governments alike. Only through a concerted and sustained effort can we hope to protect the integrity of our democratic processes and safeguard the well-being of our communities.

Economic Justice for All
Addressing Inequality and Promoting Opportunity

Let's explore strategies for addressing economic inequality, promoting opportunity, and creating a more just and equitable society.

The chasm between the wealthy and the impoverished continues to widen in many nations, creating a landscape of economic inequality that threatens social stability and undermines the very foundations of a just and equitable society. This essay examines strategies for addressing this pervasive issue, focusing on policies and initiatives designed to promote opportunity, reduce disparities, and ultimately foster Economic Justice for All. Understanding the multifaceted nature of economic inequality is crucial before exploring potential solutions. It's not simply a matter of income; it encompasses disparities in wealth, access to education and healthcare, and even the disproportionate impact of environmental hazards on marginalized communities. Ignoring these complexities allows the problem to fester, perpetuating cycles of poverty and limiting the potential of individuals and communities.

One of the most fundamental strategies for addressing economic inequality is through progressive taxation. This system, where higher earners pay a larger percentage of their income in taxes, provides the resources necessary to fund social safety nets and public services that disproportionately benefit low-income individuals and families. Revenue generated through progressive taxation can be channeled into programs like affordable housing, food assistance, and childcare subsidies, providing a crucial lifeline for those struggling to make ends meet. Furthermore, it can be used to invest in education and job training programs, empowering individuals to acquire the skills and knowledge needed to climb the economic ladder. However, the effectiveness of progressive taxation hinges on its implementation. Loopholes must be closed, tax evasion must be aggressively pursued, and international cooperation is necessary to prevent multinational corporations from shifting profits to tax havens.

Beyond taxation, investing in education provides a powerful avenue for upward mobility. Ensuring equal access to quality education, from early childhood programs to higher education, is paramount. This includes funding under-resourced schools, providing scholarships and grants for low-income students, and investing in teacher training and development. Universal pre-kindergarten programs, for example, have been shown to have long-term positive effects on children's academic performance and future earning potential, helping to break the cycle of poverty from an early age. Moreover, education must be tailored to meet the needs of a changing economy. Vocational training programs and apprenticeships can provide individuals with the skills required for in-demand jobs, offering a pathway to stable employment and economic security. Addressing the rising cost of higher education is also critical. Student loan debt has become a significant burden for many graduates, hindering their ability to save for retirement, purchase homes, and invest in their futures. Exploring alternative funding models for higher education, such as tuition-free or debt-free college programs, can help to alleviate this burden and ensure that higher education is accessible to all, regardless of their socioeconomic background.

Another critical element in promoting economic justice is strengthening labor protections and empowering workers. This includes raising the minimum wage to a living wage, ensuring fair pay for women and minority workers, and protecting the right to organize and collectively bargain. A living wage allows workers to meet their basic needs, reducing reliance on public assistance and stimulating local economies. Addressing the gender pay gap and racial wage gap is crucial to ensuring that all workers are compensated fairly for their contributions. Strengthening unions and protecting workers' rights to organize empowers them to negotiate for better wages, benefits, and working conditions, leading to a more equitable distribution of wealth and power. Furthermore, policies that promote workplace flexibility, such as paid family leave and affordable childcare, can help to alleviate the burden on working families, particularly single-parent households, and enable more individuals to participate fully in the workforce.

The role of government in regulating the economy also cannot be overlooked. Unfettered capitalism can lead to excessive concentration of wealth and power, creating an uneven playing field and stifling competition. Strong regulatory oversight is needed to prevent monopolies, protect consumers, and ensure fair business practices. This includes regulating the financial industry to prevent predatory lending and speculative bubbles, enforcing antitrust laws to promote competition, and regulating environmental pollution to protect public health and ensure environmental sustainability. Furthermore, government investment in infrastructure, such as transportation, energy, and communication networks, can create jobs, stimulate economic growth, and improve the quality of life for all citizens.

Finally, addressing systemic biases and discriminatory practices is essential to achieving Economic Justice for All. This includes combating discrimination in housing, employment, and access to credit, and promoting diversity and inclusion in all sectors of society. Policies such as affirmative action, while controversial, can help to level the playing field and ensure that individuals from historically disadvantaged groups have an equal opportunity to succeed. Furthermore, promoting financial literacy and providing access to affordable financial services can help to empower individuals to manage their finances effectively and build wealth. This includes providing access to credit counseling, savings programs, and affordable banking services.

In conclusion, achieving Economic Justice for All requires a comprehensive and multifaceted approach. It demands a commitment to progressive taxation, investment in education, strengthening labor protections, government regulation, and addressing systemic biases. These strategies are not mutually exclusive; rather, they are interconnected and mutually reinforcing. Implementing these policies will undoubtedly face resistance from powerful interests who benefit from the status quo. However, the pursuit of economic justice is not merely a matter of fairness; it is essential for creating a more prosperous, stable, and equitable society for all. By addressing inequality and promoting opportunity, we can

unlock the full potential of individuals and communities, fostering a society where everyone has the chance to thrive and contribute to the common good. The future of our societies depends on our willingness to tackle this challenge head-on and create an economy that works for everyone, not just a select few.

Let's discuss the importance of fair wages, affordable healthcare, and access to education.

THE CORNERSTONES OF A JUST ECONOMY
Fair Wages, Healthcare, and Education

A vibrant and prosperous society is not merely defined by its Gross Domestic Product or its technological advancements, but also by the equitable distribution of its resources and opportunities. A society riddled with stark inequalities, where a select few amass immense wealth while the majority struggles to meet basic needs, is inherently unstable and unsustainable. To foster genuine progress and social cohesion, we must prioritize policies that address the root causes of inequality and build a foundation of economic security for all. Central to this endeavor are three crucial pillars: fair wages, affordable healthcare, and access to education.

Firstly, **fair wages** are not simply a matter of economic justice, but a fundamental prerequisite for a functioning economy. When wages stagnate or fail to keep pace with inflation and productivity gains, purchasing power erodes, leading to decreased consumer demand and ultimately hindering economic growth. A living wage, on the other hand, empowers individuals and families to meet their basic needs, participate more fully in the economy, and invest in their future. This translates into increased spending, job creation, and a more robust national economy.

The argument that raising wages will lead to job losses has been repeatedly debunked by empirical evidence. Studies on minimum wage increases in various cities and states have shown minimal negative impacts on employment, and in some cases, even positive effects as increased consumer spending stimulates demand and creates new opportunities. Furthermore, fair wages can reduce employee turnover, leading to cost savings for businesses through reduced training and recruitment expenses. By ensuring that workers receive a fair share of the wealth they help create, we not only enhance their economic well-being, but also foster a more productive and equitable society.

Beyond the immediate impact on individual livelihoods, fair wages have broader societal implications. They can reduce reliance on public assistance programs, freeing up resources for other critical investments in education, infrastructure, and public safety. They can also contribute to a more stable and secure society by reducing crime rates and fostering a sense of shared prosperity. In short, fair wages are not just good economics, they are good social policy.

Secondly, **affordable healthcare** is a non-negotiable component of a just economy. Access to quality healthcare should not be determined by one's income or employment status. When individuals are forced to choose between seeking medical treatment and paying for basic necessities, the consequences can be devastating, both for the individual and for society as a whole. Preventative care is often foregone, leading to more serious and costly health problems down the line. Chronic illnesses go unmanaged, reducing productivity and increasing healthcare costs in the long run.

Countries with universal healthcare systems, such as Canada, the United Kingdom, and many European nations, have demonstrated that it is possible to provide comprehensive healthcare to all citizens at a lower cost per capita than the United States, while also achieving better health outcomes. These systems often employ a combination of public and private providers, but the key is that access is guaranteed to everyone, regardless of their ability to pay.

Investing in affordable healthcare is not just a moral imperative, it is also a sound economic strategy. A healthy workforce is a productive workforce. When people have access to timely and quality healthcare, they are less likely to miss work due to illness, and they are more likely to be able to contribute fully to the economy. Furthermore, affordable healthcare reduces the burden of medical debt, allowing individuals and families to invest in their education, start businesses, and contribute to economic growth.

Finally, **access to education** is the great equalizer, providing individuals with the skills and knowledge they need to succeed in the modern economy. Education empowers individuals to climb the socioeconomic ladder, break the cycle of poverty, and contribute meaningfully to society. However, in many societies, access to quality education is highly unequal, with children from low-income families often attending under-resourced schools and facing significant barriers to higher education.

Investing in education, from early childhood programs to higher education and vocational training, is crucial for promoting economic mobility and reducing inequality. High-quality early childhood education provides children with a strong foundation for future learning, while affordable higher education allows individuals to acquire the skills and credentials they need to compete in the global marketplace. Vocational training programs equip individuals with the practical skills and knowledge needed for in-demand jobs, providing a pathway to economic security for those who may not pursue a traditional four-year degree.

Successful Economic Policies that Reduced Inequality:

While the challenges of inequality are complex and multifaceted, history offers examples of successful economic policies that have demonstrably reduced inequality and fostered shared prosperity.

THE NEW DEAL (UNITED STATES): Implemented in response to the Great Depression, the New Deal employed a range of policies aimed at providing relief, recovery, and reform. Programs like the Works Progress Administration (WPA) and the Civilian Conservation Corps (CCC) provided millions of jobs, while Social Security provided a safety net for the elderly and unemployed. These policies not only alleviated immediate suffering but also laid the foundation for a more equitable and prosperous society in the decades that followed.

THE POST-WAR SOCIAL DEMOCRATIC MODEL (SCANDINAVIA): Countries like Sweden, Denmark, and Norway adopted a social democratic model characterized by strong social safety nets, progressive taxation, and collective bargaining. These policies led to high levels of social mobility, low levels of poverty, and a relatively egalitarian distribution of income. While these countries have faced challenges in recent years, their success in reducing inequality serves as a valuable lesson for other nations.

LAND REFORM IN EAST ASIA: In the aftermath of World War II, several East Asian countries, including South Korea and Taiwan, implemented significant land reforms that redistributed land from wealthy landowners to tenant farmers. This empowered rural populations, boosted agricultural productivity, and laid the foundation for rapid economic development.

THE EXPANSION OF THE EARNED INCOME TAX CREDIT (EITC) IN THE UNITED STATES: The EITC is a refundable tax credit for low- to moderate-income working individuals and families. Studies have shown that the EITC is an effective tool for reducing poverty and encouraging work, particularly among single mothers. By supplementing the earnings of low-wage workers, the EITC helps to ensure that work pays and provides a pathway out of poverty.

These examples demonstrate that governments can play a proactive role in reducing inequality and promoting shared prosperity through a combination of progressive taxation, robust social safety nets, investments in education and healthcare, and policies that empower workers and promote fair wages.

In conclusion, building a just and equitable economy requires a multifaceted approach that prioritizes the well-being of all members of society. Fair wages, affordable healthcare, and access to education are not merely desirable goals, but essential cornerstones of a thriving and sustainable economy. By embracing these principles and implementing policies that promote them, we can create a society where everyone has the opportunity to reach their full potential and contribute to the common good. The challenges are significant, but the rewards of a more just and equitable society are immeasurable.

A GLOBAL AWAKENING

Building Solidarity and Defending Human Rights on the Front Lines

Let's analyze the importance of international cooperation, solidarity, and human rights activism.

In an increasingly interconnected world, the echoes of injustice in one corner reverberate across the globe, forcing us to confront the uncomfortable truth that our fates are inextricably intertwined. This realization, this burgeoning awareness of our shared humanity and the precariousness of fundamental rights, marks the beginning of a global awakening. It's an era demanding not passive observation, but active participation in building solidarity and defending human rights on the front lines, wherever they may be. This essay will examine the critical importance of international cooperation, the power of unwavering solidarity, and the vital role of human rights activism in forging a more just and equitable future for all.

The foundation of a truly just global order rests upon the bedrock of international cooperation. No single nation, however powerful, can effectively address the complex challenges facing humanity today. From climate change and pandemics to economic inequality and political instability, these are global problems demanding global solutions. Ignoring borders and transcending national interests, international cooperation facilitates the sharing of resources, knowledge, and expertise. Through collaborative efforts like the United Nations, international treaties, and cross-border partnerships, nations can work together to establish universal standards, enforce accountability, and provide essential humanitarian assistance. The Sustainable Development Goals (SDGs), for example, represent a comprehensive roadmap for global progress, requiring collaborative action across diverse sectors to eradicate poverty, promote education, and ensure environmental sustainability. Without genuine cooperation, these ambitious goals remain elusive, and the potential for conflict and instability increases exponentially.

Beyond formal agreements and governmental collaboration, genuine solidarity forms the very lifeblood of the human rights movement. Solidarity transcends geographical boundaries, cultural differences, and political affiliations. It is the unwavering commitment to stand alongside those whose rights are being violated, to amplify their voices, and to offer tangible support. This can manifest in a multitude of ways, from participating in peaceful protests and signing online petitions to donating to humanitarian organizations and advocating for policy changes. The power of solidarity lies in its ability to break down isolation and empower marginalized communities. Consider the global response to the Black Lives Matter movement. Triggered by instances of police brutality in the United States, the movement resonated globally, sparking protests and conversations about systemic racism and discrimination in countless countries. This outpouring of solidarity demonstrated the interconnectedness of struggles for racial justice and the power of collective action to demand meaningful change. By recognizing our shared humanity and acting in unison, we can create a powerful force for positive transformation.

At the heart of this global awakening lies the courageous work of human rights activists. Often working in dangerous and challenging environments, these individuals and organizations are the watchdogs of democracy, the voices of the voiceless, and the frontline defenders of fundamental freedoms. They document human rights violations, provide legal assistance to victims, advocate for policy reforms, and challenge oppressive regimes. Human rights activists are essential for holding perpetrators accountable and ensuring that international human rights laws are upheld. Their tireless efforts often come at a great personal cost, facing threats, intimidation, and even violence. The work of organizations like Amnesty International, Human Rights Watch, and Reporters Without Borders provides invaluable documentation and advocacy, shining a spotlight on abuses and pressuring governments to take action. Furthermore, the rise of citizen journalism and social media activism has empowered individuals to document and disseminate information, bypassing traditional media channels and holding power to account in real-time. The courage and dedication of these activists serve as an inspiration and a reminder that even in the face of overwhelming adversity, change is possible.

However, the path towards a truly just and equitable world is not without its obstacles. The rise of nationalism, populism, and authoritarianism in recent years poses a significant threat to international cooperation and the protection of human rights. These ideologies often prioritize national interests over global solidarity, demonize minority groups, and undermine democratic institutions. Misinformation and disinformation campaigns further erode trust in institutions and sow division within societies, making it more difficult to address complex challenges. Moreover, economic inequality remains a pervasive issue, fueling social unrest and creating conditions where basic human rights are systematically denied to large segments of the population.

Overcoming these challenges requires a multi-faceted approach. First, we must strengthen international institutions and promote multilateralism as the most effective means of addressing global challenges. This includes reforming the UN to make it more representative and effective, strengthening international legal frameworks, and fostering greater cooperation on issues like climate change, trade, and migration. Second, we must actively combat misinformation and disinformation by promoting media literacy, supporting independent journalism, and holding social media companies accountable for the content that is shared on their platforms. Third, we must address economic inequality by implementing progressive tax policies, investing in education and job training, and strengthening social safety nets. Finally, and perhaps most importantly, we must cultivate a culture of empathy, tolerance, and respect for diversity. This requires promoting human rights education in schools and communities, fostering intercultural dialogue, and challenging prejudice and discrimination in all its forms.

The global awakening we are witnessing is a call to action. It is a recognition that we are all interconnected and that the defense of human rights is a shared responsibility. By strengthening international cooperation, building solidarity, and supporting human rights activism, we can create a world where everyone has the opportunity to live with dignity, freedom, and justice. The challenges are significant, but the potential rewards are immeasurable. The future of humanity depends on our willingness to embrace our shared humanity and to stand together on the front lines, defending human rights for all. The time for complacency is over. The time for action is now. Let us answer the call and build a brighter future, together

THE GLOBAL GUARDIANS

Defending Democracy
And Promoting Human Rights in an
Age of Uncertainty

Democracy and human rights, the cornerstones of a just and equitable world, are under increasing pressure in the 21st century. From the rise of authoritarian regimes to the spread of disinformation and the erosion of civil liberties, the challenges are multifaceted and complex. In this environment, the role of international organizations, non-governmental organizations (NGOs), and individual citizens becomes paramount in defending democratic principles and promoting universal human rights. These actors, working in concert or independently, act as global guardians, holding power accountable, supporting vulnerable populations, and advocating for a more just and free world.

International organizations, such as the United Nations (UN), play a crucial role in establishing international norms and providing a platform for collective action. The UN's Universal Declaration of Human Rights, adopted in 1948, remains a foundational document, outlining the fundamental rights and freedoms to which every individual is entitled. The UN's Human Rights Council investigates human rights violations, monitors compliance with international treaties, and provides technical assistance to states seeking to improve their human rights record. However, the effectiveness of these institutions is often hampered by political considerations, national interests, and the power dynamics within the international system. Decisions can be vetoed, investigations blocked, and resolutions watered down, limiting the UN's ability to act decisively in the face of egregious human rights abuses.

Complementing the work of international organizations are NGOs, which operate on the ground, often with greater flexibility and independence. These organizations, ranging from large, internationally recognized entities like Amnesty International and Human Rights Watch to smaller, locally-based groups, play a vital role in monitoring human rights violations, providing legal aid to victims, advocating for policy changes, and educating the public about democratic values. Amnesty International, for example, mobilizes public pressure to release prisoners of conscience and end torture, while Human Rights Watch investigates and reports on a wide range of human rights abuses around the world. These organizations often work in dangerous environments, facing threats and intimidation from authoritarian regimes. Their dedication to uncovering the truth and advocating for justice is essential in holding perpetrators accountable and providing support to those who are most vulnerable.

Beyond the actions of formal organizations, the power of individual citizens cannot be underestimated. From activists and journalists to ordinary individuals who stand up for their rights, the collective voice of the people is a powerful force for change. Social media has become a crucial tool for organizing protests, disseminating information, and documenting human rights abuses, often circumventing state censorship and providing a platform for marginalized voices. Individual citizens can also contribute by supporting NGOs, engaging in political activism, and holding their own governments accountable for their human rights record. The courage of whistleblowers, who risk their personal safety to expose corruption and human rights violations, is particularly crucial in holding power accountable.

Throughout history, there have been numerous success stories of activism and resistance against authoritarianism, demonstrating the power of collective action and the enduring appeal of democratic ideals. The Solidarity movement in Poland, for example, played a pivotal role in dismantling the communist regime through non-violent resistance, strikes, and public demonstrations. The movement's success was due in part to its strong grassroots base, its ability to mobilize public support, and its international solidarity networks. Similarly, the anti-apartheid movement in South Africa, through decades of sustained activism, boycotts, sanctions, and international pressure, eventually led to the end of racial segregation and the establishment of a democratic government. These examples demonstrate that even the most entrenched authoritarian regimes can be challenged and overthrown by a determined and united citizenry.

More recently, the Arab Spring uprisings, while ultimately yielding mixed results, showcased the transformative power of popular movements in demanding democratic reforms and challenging oppressive regimes. The protests, driven by a desire for freedom, dignity, and economic opportunity, swept across the Middle East and North Africa, inspiring millions to take to the streets and demand change. While many of these uprisings were met with violent repression, they demonstrated the enduring yearning for democracy and the willingness of ordinary people to risk their lives for a better future.

The ongoing struggle for democracy and human rights in Belarus provides another powerful example of resistance against authoritarianism. Following the disputed 2020 presidential election, widespread protests erupted across the country, demanding free and fair elections and an end to President Lukashenko's long and repressive reign. Despite facing brutal crackdowns, arrests, and torture, the Belarusian people have continued to resist, organizing demonstrations, using social media to coordinate activities, and demanding accountability for human rights abuses. The resilience and determination of the Belarusian people serve as an inspiration to democrats around the world and highlight the importance of international solidarity in supporting those who are fighting for freedom and justice.

However, it is important to acknowledge that the fight for democracy and human rights is not always successful. In many countries, authoritarian regimes have managed to consolidate their power, suppress dissent, and restrict civil liberties. The rise of populism and nationalism in many Western democracies has also led to the erosion of democratic norms and institutions, threatening the very foundations of liberal democracy. Disinformation and propaganda campaigns, often spread through social media, can undermine public trust in institutions and polarize societies, making it more difficult to build consensus and address pressing social problems.

In conclusion, defending democracy and promoting human rights requires a multi-faceted approach, involving the concerted efforts of international organizations, NGOs, and individual citizens. While international organizations provide a framework for international cooperation and norm-setting, NGOs play a crucial role in monitoring human rights violations, providing support to victims, and advocating for policy changes. Ultimately, however, the power rests with individual citizens who, through their activism, resistance, and unwavering commitment to democratic values, can hold power accountable and create a more just and equitable world. The success stories of activism and resistance against authoritarianism serve as a reminder that even in the face of overwhelming odds, the pursuit of freedom and justice is a cause worth fighting for. The global guardians, in their various forms, must continue to stand vigilant, defend democratic principles, and promote universal human rights, ensuring that the promise of a free and just world remains within reach. The challenges are significant, but the stakes are too high to remain silent or indifferent. The future of democracy and human rights depends on the collective action of individuals and organizations around the world who are committed to making a difference.

The World We Can Choose
A Call to Action

A powerful call to action, urging readers to become engaged citizens and to work towards a more just, democratic, and sustainable world.

We stand at a precipice, a pivotal moment in history where the choices we make today will irrevocably shape the world of tomorrow. From the melting glaciers to the widening chasms of inequality, the challenges facing humanity are both daunting and demanding. Yet, despair is not an option. Complacency is not permissible. This is not a time for passive observation, but a clarion call to action, urging each and every one of us to become engaged citizens, proactive participants in the construction of a more just, democratic, and sustainable world.

The very notion that we *can* choose the world we inhabit is itself a revolutionary idea. It flies in the face of cynicism, the pervasive feeling that our individual actions are insignificant against the vast, complex machinery of global challenges. It rejects the notion that we are merely passengers on a runaway train, hurtling towards an inevitable and potentially devastating future. Instead, it empowers us, reminding us that the future is not a fixed entity, but a malleable creation, sculpted by the collective will of humanity.

But what does it mean to be an engaged citizen in this context? It begins with awareness, a deep and critical understanding of the complex issues that plague our world. We must move beyond superficial headlines and delve into the root causes of climate change, poverty, inequality, and injustice. This requires a commitment to education, to seeking out reliable information, and to critically evaluating the narratives presented to us by various sources. We must understand the science, the economics, and the social factors that underpin these challenges.

Awareness, however, is only the first step. It must be followed by action. This can take many forms, tailored to individual skills, passions, and circumstances. For some, it might mean becoming politically active, advocating for policies that promote sustainability, social justice, and democratic reform. This could involve writing to elected officials, participating in peaceful protests, or supporting organizations working on these issues. It might also mean running for office oneself, becoming a voice for change from within the system.

For others, action might focus on making conscious consumer choices. By supporting businesses that prioritize ethical and sustainable practices, we can send a powerful message to the market. By reducing our consumption, reusing materials, and recycling diligently, we can minimize our environmental impact. By choosing to support fair trade initiatives, we can help to ensure that producers in developing countries receive a fair price for their goods.

Beyond these individual actions, we must also cultivate a sense of community and collaboration. The challenges we face are too complex and too interconnected to be solved in isolation. We must work together, across divides of culture, ideology, and geography, to find common ground and to build solutions that benefit all of humanity. This requires open dialogue, empathy, and a willingness to compromise. It demands that we listen to and learn from those with different perspectives, even when those perspectives challenge our own deeply held beliefs.

Creating a more just and democratic world also requires a constant vigilance against the forces that seek to undermine these values. We must defend freedom of speech, freedom of the press, and the right to assembly. We must challenge corruption, protect minority rights, and ensure that everyone has access to education, healthcare, and economic opportunities. We must be willing to stand up for those who are marginalized and oppressed, and to fight against all forms of discrimination and prejudice.

Furthermore, building a sustainable future demands a fundamental shift in our relationship with the natural world. We must move beyond a purely anthropocentric view, recognizing that we are just one species among many, and that our survival depends on the health and well-being of the entire planet. This requires a commitment to protecting biodiversity, conserving natural resources, and transitioning to a clean energy economy. It also requires a profound respect for the inherent value of nature, a recognition that the natural world is not merely a resource to be exploited, but a source of beauty, wonder, and inspiration.

Ultimately, the world we can choose is a world built on hope, resilience, and a unwavering commitment to the common good. It is a world where everyone has the opportunity to thrive, where the environment is protected, and where peace and justice prevail. It is a world that may seem distant and unattainable, but one that is within our reach if we are willing to work for it. This is not just a utopian dream; it is a practical imperative. For the alternative – a world of increasing inequality, environmental degradation, and social unrest – is simply not sustainable.

Let us, therefore, embrace the challenge before us. Let us become engaged citizens, active participants in the creation of a better future. Let us choose a world of justice, democracy, and sustainability. The time to act is now. The future is ours to shape. Let us shape it wisely. Let us shape it together. Let us shape it for the benefit of all.

The weight of our present reality presses down with undeniable force. From the escalating impacts of climate change to the persistent inequalities that fracture our societies, the challenges we face are monumental and demand immediate attention. Yet, even in the face of such daunting circumstances, succumbing to despair is not an option. Now, more than ever, we must cling to the unwavering power of hope, cultivate the resilience to overcome setbacks, and harness the transformative potential of collective action.

Hope, in this context, is not a naive optimism that ignores the gravity of the situation. Instead, it is a conscious choice to believe in the possibility of a better future, a future where humanity has risen to meet its greatest challenges and forged a more sustainable and equitable world. This hope is fueled by the countless examples of progress already achieved: the advancements in renewable energy technologies, the growing global awareness of social injustice, and the inspiring movements of individuals and communities working tirelessly to create positive change. Consider the remarkable story of the reforestation efforts in the Loess Plateau of China, where degraded land has been transformed into a thriving ecosystem through collaborative action and a long-term vision. This demonstrates the incredible restorative power we possess when united by a common goal.

However, hope without action is merely wishful thinking. Resilience is the vital bridge between aspiration and achievement. It is the capacity to adapt, persevere, and learn from both our successes and our failures. The path to a sustainable and just future will undoubtedly be fraught with obstacles. There will be moments of discouragement, setbacks that test our resolve, and powerful forces resistant to change. But it is in these moments that resilience becomes paramount. We must draw strength from our shared values, learn from our past mistakes, and continue to innovate and adapt in the face of adversity. The environmental activists who continue to protest despite facing arrest and intimidation exemplify this resilience, demonstrating an unwavering commitment to their cause.

Ultimately, the scale of the challenges we face necessitates a fundamental shift towards collective action. No single individual, organization, or nation can solve these problems alone. We must break down the silos that separate us and work together across borders, ideologies, and sectors. This requires fostering genuine dialogue, building trust, and creating inclusive platforms for collaboration. Collective action means supporting community-led initiatives, advocating for policy changes, and holding our leaders accountable. It means recognizing that every individual has a role to play, and that even small acts of solidarity can contribute to a larger movement for change. Think of the global movement for climate justice, bringing together activists, scientists, and concerned citizens from all corners of the world to demand urgent action from governments and corporations. Their collective voice is a powerful force for change.

Let us be clear: the urgency of the situation cannot be overstated. The window of opportunity to avert the most catastrophic consequences of climate change is rapidly closing. The inequalities that plague our societies continue to fuel conflict and instability. We can no longer afford to delay or postpone meaningful action. Incremental changes are insufficient; we need bold and transformative solutions that address the root causes of these problems. This requires a fundamental shift in our values, our priorities, and our systems. We must move away from a model of unsustainable consumption and prioritize the well-being of both people and the planet.

The time for complacency is over. The future of humanity depends on our willingness to embrace hope, cultivate resilience, and act collectively with courage and determination. Let us rise to the occasion and create a world worthy of future generations. Let us commit to building a future where sustainability, justice, and peace prevail. Let us choose action, choose hope, and choose a better world, together.

THE MIND REVOLUTION
Forging a Future of Sustainability, Justice, and Peace

The weight of the world presses down, a confluence of crises demanding immediate and profound change. The window of opportunity to avert the most catastrophic consequences of climate change is rapidly closing, a chilling reminder of our collective inaction. The inequalities that plague our societies continue to fester, fueling conflict and instability that threaten the very fabric of human connection. We can no longer afford to delay or postpone meaningful action, clinging to the comfort of the familiar while the ground crumbles beneath our feet. Incremental changes, polite adjustments to unsustainable systems, are simply insufficient. They are Band-Aids on a gaping wound, offering the illusion of progress while failing to address the underlying infection. We need bold and transformative solutions that address the root causes of these problems, solutions that reach beyond the superficial and challenge the very foundations upon which our world is built.

This imperative for radical change necessitates a fundamental shift, a revolution not of armies and battlefields, but of the mind. It requires a profound re-evaluation of our values, our priorities, and the systems we have created. We must move away from a model of unsustainable consumption, a relentless drive for economic growth that prioritizes profit over people and planet. We must dismantle the structures that perpetuate inequality and oppression, ensuring that all members of society have the opportunity to thrive and contribute to a shared future. This is not merely a call for practical action; it is a call for a profound transformation of consciousness.

The prevailing mindset, shaped by generations of ingrained habits and societal conditioning, is the very obstacle we must overcome. We have been taught to value competition over collaboration, material wealth over spiritual well-being, short-term gain over long-term sustainability. This mindset, driven by ego and self-interest, has led us down a path of environmental degradation, social injustice, and ultimately, self-destruction. To forge a different future, we must cultivate a new way of thinking, a new way of being.

This "Mind Revolution" begins with an honest and unflinching self-assessment. We must confront our own complicity in perpetuating the systems we seek to change. We must examine our own biases, prejudices, and assumptions, and challenge the narratives that have shaped our understanding of the world. This is not always a comfortable process. It requires vulnerability, humility, and a willingness to question our deeply held beliefs. But it is a necessary process if we are to break free from the chains of the past and create a more just and sustainable future.

Furthermore, this revolution demands that we cultivate empathy and compassion. We must learn to see the world through the eyes of others, to understand the perspectives of those who are different from us, and to recognize the inherent dignity and worth of every human being. This empathy must extend beyond our immediate circle, encompassing all living things and the planet itself. We must recognize that we are all interconnected, that our fates are inextricably linked, and that the well-being of one is dependent on the well-being of all.

The time for complacency is over. The future of humanity depends on our willingness to embrace hope, to cultivate resilience, and to act collectively with courage and determination. Hope is not a passive sentiment; it is an active choice, a deliberate act of defiance against despair. It is the fuel that ignites our passion, the compass that guides our actions, and the unwavering belief that a better world is possible.

Resilience is the ability to bounce back from adversity, to learn from our mistakes, and to persevere in the face of challenges. It is the strength that allows us to keep moving forward, even when the path ahead seems daunting and uncertain.

And finally, we must act collectively. No single individual, no single organization, can solve these problems alone. We must work together, across borders, across cultures, and across ideological divides, to build a global movement for change. This requires a spirit of collaboration, a willingness to compromise, and a shared commitment to creating a world where sustainability, justice, and peace prevail.

Let us rise to the occasion and create a world worthy of future generations. Let us commit to building a future where sustainability is not just a buzzword, but a way of life; where justice is not just a legal concept, but a lived reality; and where peace is not just the absence of war, but the presence of harmony and understanding. This is not a utopian dream; it is a practical necessity. The challenges we face are immense, but so too is our potential. By embracing the Mind Revolution, by transforming our values, our priorities, and our systems, we can create a future that is not just sustainable, but truly thriving. Let us choose action, choose hope, and choose a better world, together. Let the revolution begin, not in the streets, but in the minds and hearts of This is our moment. This is our responsibility. This is our chance to build a legacy of which we can be proud. The future is not predetermined; it is a blank canvas, waiting for us to paint it with the colors of hope, resilience, and collective action.

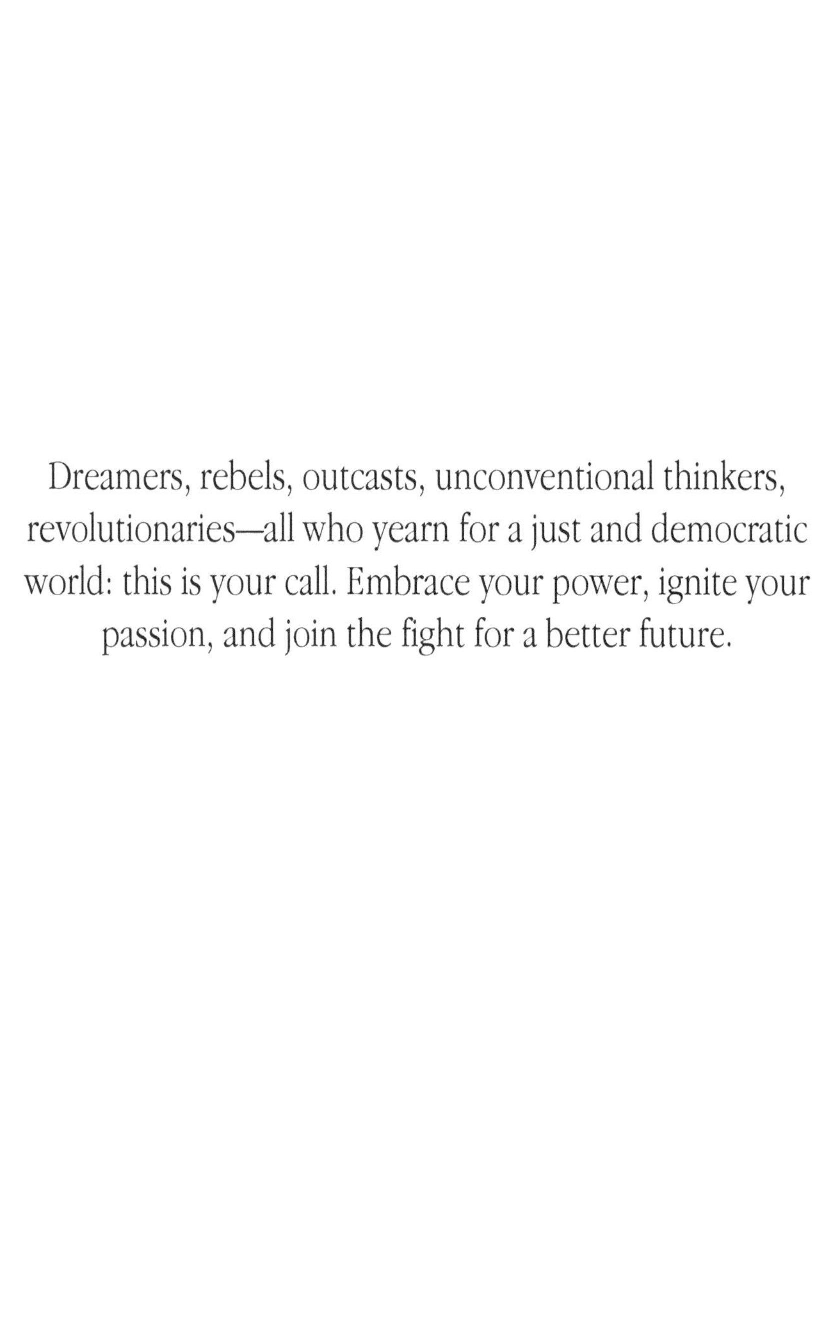

Dreamers, rebels, outcasts, unconventional thinkers, revolutionaries—all who yearn for a just and democratic world: this is your call. Embrace your power, ignite your passion, and join the fight for a better future.